SOLDIER
FOR LIFE

12Th SMA

Jack L Tilley

SOLDIER FOR LIFE

LEADER LESSONS FROM THE 12TH SERGEANT MAJOR OF THE ARMY JACK L. TILLEY

SMA JACK L. TILLEY
(U.S. ARMY, RET.)
AND
CSM DANIEL. K. ELDER
(U.S. ARMY, RET.)

NCO Historical Society

NCO HISTORICAL SOCIETY,
TEXAS

Title: Soldier for Life
Subtitle: Leader Lessons from the 12th Sergeant Major of the Army Jack L. Tilley
Authors: Jack L. Tilley and Daniel K. Elder

NCO Historical Society
P.O. Box 1341
Temple, TX 76503
www.ncohistory.com

I have tried to recreate events, locales and conversations from my memories of them. To maintain their anonymity in some instances I have changed the names of individuals and places. I may have changed some identifying characteristics and details such as physical properties, occupations, and places of residence.

Contact the NCO Historical Society for changes or updates at info@ncohistory.com.

All photographs are property of the author, unless otherwise noted.

Cover photograph courtesy Department of Defense.
Sergeant Major of the Army rank insignia image courtesy The Institute of Heraldry.

ISBN-10: 0-9963181-1-9
ISBN-13: 978-0-9963181-1-2

Published in the United States of America
2nd Edition

Dedication

To my wife and the rock of my family, Gloria;
Through Brian and Kevin and Tanja;
For Destiny and Jordan

With Love.

Contents

Preface

This book was written in recognition of the sacrifices Soldiers make while fighting our country's wars and I am thankful for the training and leadership required to develop our formations. Within our military structure, more than 80 percent of the force are enlisted personnel. These men and woman selflessly serve in support of the U.S. Constitution and protect the rights of all Americans. They represent the best our great country has to offer!

Since 14 June 1775, Soldiers have defended freedom and fought on behalf of the American way of life. All of our forces—heavy and light, active, Guard, and Reserve—share the heritage of the Continental Army. The Army's Birthday celebrates this great institution and reminds us that there is no greater profession than the Profession of Arms and no greater job than that of serving our nation.

For more than 240 years the U.S. military has taken young men and women and provided them with structure and discipline, in turn creating a global superpower. I was and remain a believer of the principles of this institution, which has shaped the foundation of our great nation. Honor, Courage, Duty, and Sacrifice are embedded in the ethos of the men and women who serve our great nation.

The good order and discipline instilled in our Soldiers by the U.S. Army were instrumental in formation of the book and my life—an institution that instills camaraderie and diversity within the ranks, despite differences of the greater society. The lessons through my over 35 years of service as an American Soldier assisted my development as I grew. The education the Army provided me helped with the handling the trials, tribulations and traumatic impact of war. These reflections gave me a greater appreciation of my family and friends and the observations provided a review of issues and circumstances that were psychologically buried.

ACKNOWLEDGEMENTS

There are too many great and wonderful people that I have come in contact with throughout my career, I cannot emphasize the amount of thanks and gratitude that I have for them. I wish to thank my coauthor Dan Elder, Johnny Myers, fellow trooper Dan Thompson, editors Brett Keener and Joe Sumlin, and cover designer Carl Graves of Extended Imagery. Most importantly I want to thank the officers, noncommissioned officers and Soldiers that have contributed to my development, as well as my family; my wife Gloria, sons Brian and Kevin, daughter-in-law Tanja, and granddaughters Destiny and Jordan. This book conveys a few of my lessons for overcoming adversity and what I hope will be self-development and enhancing leadership opportunities for the reader. These lessons strengthened my resolve and philosophy of ensuring my subordinates and superiors were never lacking the resources needed to accomplish the mission.

Sgt. Maj. of the Army Jack L. Tilley,
U.S. Army, Retired
12th Sergeant Major of the Army

Sergeant Major of the Army

Sergeant Major of the Army. This is the senior sergeant major grade and designates the senior enlisted position of the Army. The sergeant major in this position serves as the senior enlisted adviser and consultant to the CSA.

—*para. 2-18, Army Regulation 600–20, Army Command Policy*

The SMA is appointed by the Chief of Staff, Army (CSA) and serves at the discretion of the Secretary of the Army (SA). As the senior enlisted advisor to the CSA, the SMA has general oversight of all CSM and SGM Programs. The SMA has a direct role in the nominative CSM and/or SGM process and serves, concurrent with the CSA, as the approval authority for CSM slates.

—*para. 7-3, Army Regulation 614-200, Enlisted Assignments and Utilization Management*

PROLOGUE

War Changes Everything

July 11, 1967

Soldiers do not disobey orders. Well, good soldiers don't disobey orders—at least that's what they taught me. But I just had, and there was nothing I could do about it now but fire this damn machine gun.

I could not imagine at the time that this would be a defining moment in a military career that would span almost thirty-six years and influence generations of soldiers; I was only focused on saving my sergeant. Little did I know when I enlisted that I would be surrounded by outstanding soldiers during moments like this, great people who taught me some of life's most valuable lessons. Such life-shaping events often happen amid circumstances not of our choosing, and on this night, I found myself in a place where I was not supposed to be and among people that I was not supposed to be serving with. I had joined the Army with a plan—so how could things have gone off track like this, putting me in this place and under these conditions? My life was about to change. I was receiving a crash course in leadership and courage. Tonight, my sergeant would save my life.

The idea of joining the Army was born out of bragging between kids fresh out of Fort Vancouver High School in

Vancouver, Washington. Although Vietnam was in the news, I was only seventeen and hadn't thought much about the war. At the time becoming a soldier just seemed like the thing to do. It was during a trip to the local riverbank that three boyhood friends and I made the decision to join the Army. It was a plan we came up with out of the blue, a split-second decision that we had not put much thought into. We joked that it was a way out of Vancouver and that we would be able to see the world.

The following Monday we were all supposed to meet at the recruiting station; for some of the guys these proved to be only words, and ultimately only one of them, Barney Boykin, would join me. I convinced my mom to sign the papers and I was soon on my way to becoming a soldier in the United States Army. I only asked the recruiter that my pal Barney be allowed to come with me and that the Army let me jump out of airplanes. Thus, Barney and I signed contracts under the buddy plan to become something the recruiter called "Airborne Unassigned." The only thing I knew for sure was that I was on my way to Fort Lewis, Washington, to begin my career as a soldier.

My buddies and I were right about one thing: joining the army was a way to get out of Vancouver. Vietnam was about as far away from the recruiting station as I could get. By the spring of 1967, I was a private first class and yet another new guy coming to the "Quarter Cav," the 2nd platoon of A Troop of the 1st Squadron, 4th Cavalry Regiment. Our platoon was supporting an infantry company while A Troop had a platoon of infantrymen in exchange.

I was routed to the 1st Infantry Division, where I was made an assistant gunner on an armored cavalry assault vehicle (ACAV). The ACAV was a personnel carrier with the military nomenclature M113. Typically, they were outfitted with a wrap-around cupola shield for the tank commander, who had a .50-caliber M2 machine gun and front armored shield for protection. There were also two M60 machine guns, one on each side of the personnel hatch. The M60s were in gun mounts, and the gunners also had gun shields for added protection. Our platoon was equipped with three M48A3 Patton tanks and seven ACAVs, most of them without the benefit of those special kits.

I had been getting beat up riding around on search-and-destroy and route-clearance missions since I arrived, so by the time of that fateful July night I was glad to be inside the base camp with the platoon. The camp was near a rubber plantation that was originally operated by the French in a town called Quon Loi. The airfield, LZ Andy, was nothing more than a few helicopter pads located on what was once a golf course. It was a sprawling camp that was divided into platoon-sized areas for the various units based there, including our infantry company and a field artillery battery. We were assigned airfield protection duties, and as the new guy I drew guard duty on the night shift.

It was past midnight when the night exploded in a blinding flash of noise and light as one of the quad .50s on the perimeter began firing outside the wire. The gun crew had seen movement, and after verifying there were no friendlies in the area they had requested and received permission to fire. I had in the past heard the sounds of the machine guns of the ACAV and the cannon fire of the tanks, but the unexpected, continuous fire of four .50-caliber, heavy-barreled machine guns caused me to turn toward the sound, even though I couldn't see what was happening on the other side of the perimeter. Just then attackers began dropping in a hail of mortar rounds into our camp. I knew that I had to get out of the open and back to the shelter of my ACAV. As I turned to go someone from a nearby tank hollered at me to jump in the vehicle and help. Because they were short a crewman the tank commander, Staff Sergeant Harald Ahsbahs was now instructing me to load tank rounds. It was 0120 hours and it was clear that this would not be an ordinary guard shift.

Near our tank was an unused swimming pool among a complex of tile-roofed buildings. Vietcong sappers[1] had slowly and carefully crawled through the pipes of the pool's drainage system and were able to infiltrate our camp's perimeter undetected. An all-out assault had been preempted by the firing of the quad .50, but the VC were mostly in position by that point. They responded with a mortar barrage. VC snipers were up on the roofs of the buildings shooting and throwing grenades down into our vehicles. Mortars continued to explode around us for what seemed like forever. One round exploded over a helicopter crew, wounding them, while one of the quad .50 positions was taken out. Ahsbahs was following the radio traffic on the platoon frequency trying to make sense of what was happening while we hunkered down inside the tank.

As soon as the mortar attack died down we began to hear the sounds of small-arms fire. A reconnaissance response force from the battalion was outside the perimeter providing situation updates and returning fire. Our platoon leader, 1st Lt. Gordon "Jack" Smith, and platoon sergeant Sgt. 1st Class

---

[1] Sappers are engineers who typically lay mines; in Vietnam they would often use satchel charges, rocket-propelled grenades, or pipe bombs.

Daniel DeButts were each in their own vehicles when enemy fighters attacked our sector of the firebase from the front and the rear simultaneously. Vietcong were spotted inside the wire running throughout the camp, throwing satchel charges at the vehicles and artillery guns while rooftop snipers wreaked havoc across our platoon area. DeButts was killed by a sniper and Smith was seriously wounded after he picked up a satchel charge thrown in his ACAV and tried to throw it back; it went off prematurely, blowing off his arm and part of his face. The VC sappers also came equipped with rocket-propelled grenades (RPGs), and the remainder of DeButts crew were killed when their tank was struck by one. Radio contact between our beleaguered platoon and the battalion was lost and ours was the last tank that was still operational. And the battle had just begun.

As one of the senior people on the ground, Ahsbahs was now calling the shots. He saw that the attackers had blown a large hole in the perimeter and realized that was how the enemy was entering our camp. Ahsbahs told the driver to "move out" as he maneuvered the tank over to the breach and had him drive it into the gap. He told me to load up a canister round. A canister munition had about 1,280 pellets that turned the main gun on the M48 into something akin to a large shotgun. He surveyed the area, and then began to fire. *Boom!* Load canister and fire! *Boom!* Load canister and fire! *Boom!*

There may have been proper fire commands, but I don't remember, I just knew to keep loading rounds. Ahsbahs began aiming the shots at the tiled rooftops of the buildings the snipers were on, the rounds creating shards that inflicted many casualties and eventually silenced the snipers. We just kept firing and every time Ahsbahs would order "Load canister!" I would reach in to the hull to grab a fresh round and load it up and get ready for the next shot. The loader's hatch below was open so I could toss out the casings, which by now were piling up on the floor.

Half an hour went by before we had a lull in the action, and this was about when we regained radio contact with the command post. Meanwhile all around us other attacks were happening off in the distance. The nearby ARVN (Army of the Republic of Vietnam) camp in Tam Hung was coming under attack and VC positions continued to mortar our sector. As the battle raged we sometimes had enemy fire coming at us from both within and outside our perimeter. An ACAV was hit from behind with a rocket-propelled grenade and was destroyed, killing all those onboard. Eventually one of our recon platoons reached the swimming pool area; we had stopped firing earlier to allow them safe movement, and small-arms fire began to taper off.

We had been fighting for almost an hour. Sporadic shooting continued, but now there was an eerie calm in the air as smoke rose from the burning vehicles and flares from Air Force planes lit up the night. Ahsbahs told me, "Tilley, you go over and check out A25," meaning the platoon sergeant's tank. No, I thought. It wasn't fear, or maybe it was, but I decided at that moment that I wasn't going. I knew that I did not want to look in Sergeant DeButts's blown-up tank and see the carnage, so I refused. I matter-of-factly told Ahsbahs, "I'm not going." He looked at me for a long moment, and then with a hint of understanding he turned away. He never asked me a second time. Instead he said, "Get up here on the .50-cal." I worked my way through the tank to the commander's seat and grabbed the handles of the machine gun. Ahsbahs explained how he wanted me to provide him cover by "reconning by fire," shooting overhead in short bursts. He said, "Every minute or so you fire a few machine gun bursts over that way," pointing toward the wire. He hopped off the tank and ran towards A25 to check on DeButts and his crew.

At that time, I had only been in country for a few weeks, during most of which I had been an M60 assistant gunner on an ACAV. But now here I was in the early-morning darkness with my thumbs on the butterfly trigger of a heavy-barreled .50-caliber Browning machine gun. The venerable "Ma Deuce" could shoot over five hundred rounds a minute; though I had fired the gun in training, the idea that I was now about to be responsible for protecting Ahsbahs with such a weapon was exhilarating and frightening at the same time. He took off, and I only had time to squeeze off a burst or two before he was back in what seemed like only seconds. I knew by the look on his face that it was bad, and he simply told us, "Guys, it's a mess in there."

After DeButts was shot in the back of his head by a sniper the RPG round had gone through the tank from the side and hit the loader squarely in the chest. It continued on and struck the gunner near one of his legs. The only crewman to survive was the driver, who was in a separate compartment at the front of the tank. We packed up and Ahsbahs issued the order to move out. We drove across the platoon area to check on the others. To the sergeant's credit he never again mentioned my refusal to go and check on DeButts and crew.

I had confidence in the noncommissioned officers of my platoon, men like Ahsbahs. I knew to do what my sergeants told me, but at the time I had not yet learned the power of trust—my education had only just begun. We lost seven American soldiers and had twenty-two wounded that night.

S. Sergeant Harald Ahsbahs was awarded the Silver Star for his gallantry in saving our platoon. Maybe I knew it then or maybe I didn't, but war had changed my life.

[1]

Endless Summer

The phrase "what you see is what you get" suffers from overuse today and probably should be retired from the English language, but in this case it is an apt description of Jack Tilley. He seems incapable of subterfuge and comes across as open and sincere. He will tell you the truth as he understands it even if it is not what you want to hear. Sometimes the truth hurts and is not always well received and he believes honesty is the foundation that close personal and professional relationships are founded upon. Without honesty there is no trust, and without trust there is no team. The Army is a team endeavor.

—Cmd. Sgt. Maj. Jimmie Spencer, U.S. Army, Retired
former Command Sergeant Major, US Army
Special Operations Command

Summer of 1966

It's not as if I was particularly patriotic or came from a military background. My father had been drafted and spent a few years in the service but I never knew much about military life. What I did know was that I had just finished high school and I was pretty unhappy with the way things were going. I was ready for a change. I was a scrappy kid who had gone through some difficult times; my parents were divorced and I was bouncing in and out of trouble. I spent ten months in reform school and I was quickly learning how to skate by in life by doing just the minimum. Like many kids my age I was unsure of myself, or what I was going to with the rest of my life. I spent time boxing and going through the motions of life as best I could without giving a lot of thought to my future. Sports was one of the constants that helped me get through my life in Vancouver, Washington.

It was only a few months earlier, in November 1965, that the first major engagement of the Vietnam War, the Battle of the Ia Drang Valley, had begun. The United States had 120,000 troops in Vietnam at the time. I would later be one of the almost 549,000 service members present at the peak of the war around the time of the 1968 Tet Offensive. But those thoughts were far from my mind when my high school pals and I were sitting on the bank of a local river bullshitting about what we were going to do now that we were out of school. It was pretty clear that none of us had a clue when someone suggested that we join the Army. We looked around and all nodded our heads in agreement. We had heard of a program where friends could join and be stationed together, so we intended to enlist under this "buddy program." We made plans to meet up at the recruiter's office in Vancouver, and it seemed like the perfect idea—but when I got there only one actually showed up. His given name was Prentis B. Boykin Jr., but we all called him by his middle name, Barney. And so, he and I went to the recruiting office to volunteer. One of the few things I had the foresight to ask the recruiter was "could I jump out of airplanes?"

The thrill of parachuting out of a high-flying plane seemed adventurous and fun to this seventeen-year-old kid. Other than that, I had no idea what I wanted out of the Army. It was clear that I was not the only one. The Army had relied on the draft since before World War II and it was in full effect at the time. When Barney and I arrived at the induction center it was obvious that some of the men did not want to be there. For volunteers like us, this was not the best environment to be in. But we just shut our mouths and followed instructions as we went through a battery of physical and mental exams. By then I had seen enough movies to know what tanks were and the thought of serving on a heavy vehicle like that surrounded by rolled cast steel seemed like a good idea to me, so the recruiter signed us up as 11E Armored Crewmen. We were to go to basic training at Fort Lewis, Washington, and then to advanced individual tank training at Fort Knox Kentucky. Airborne qualification, Jump School—the Army's basic military parachutist training—would have to wait. It was only after basic and tank training that we would finally get the chance to earn those coveted "Jump Wings" at Fort Benning, Georgia.

Our first stop, the United States Army Personnel Center at Fort Lewis, Washington, had been established in March 1966 to meet the country's growing need for soldiers in Vietnam; the current West Coast recruit depot in Oakland, California, was overloaded. The Army Infantry Training Center at Fort Lewis was activated on May 2, 1966, and three companies began the first basic combat training cycle on July 11. Lewis was only 120 miles north by way of Interstate 5 from my Vancouver home, and Barney and I arrived on November 1, soon after the fort's first class of trainees had graduated.

Stepping off the bus at Fort Lewis was a day like few I have experienced. It was then my life took a 180-degree turn, and was the beginning of a life of change. It was also when I met Drill Sergeant Lewis. It was through him that

I had my first real introduction to what I would define as a true military professional. I don't recall if I ever knew his first name; he was simply "Yes, Drill Sergeant" to me. Lewis was a tall, thin man who did not need to demand respect—he commanded it. He did not need to yell and scream at us to get his point across. Like many men of his day he was a combat veteran.

Basic Combat Training with the 1st Basic Training Brigade at Fort Lewis was not unlike what newly enlisted soldiers go through today. I arrived like so many before us, faced with a whirl of shouting sergeants, confusing instructions, and an overabundance of push-ups for the slightest screw-up. Barney and I quickly fell in to the routine and we began to learn important skills as we went through the typical training day.

We lived in World War II–era wooden two-story buildings with about sixty soldiers per structure. (They have long since been demolished and replaced with modern facilities.) Each of us had a bunk, a locker, and a foot locker, and we would have daily inspections. We checked "butt cans" (empty mess hall cans with sand for ashtrays) and pulled "fire guard" (guard duty) as we spent the winter of 1966 in those drafty barracks and on the training ranges of Fort Lewis. I enjoyed the physical fitness training Drill Sergeant Lewis would lead us in, and our fitness test of the time consisted of five events: the mile run; the low crawl; the horizontal ladder; the dodge, run, and jump; and the grenade throw.

Drill Sergeant Lewis prepared for our lessons, conducted make-up training, gathered training aids, and maintained the trainee records. Our drill sergeant was like other men of that era, caught up in the growth of the Army and ensuring the men got the best training they could receive prior to going overseas. He lived on the second floor in the barracks during the week, and we knew that you never went towards his room. When he turned off the lights, everybody went to sleep. I would celebrate my eighteenth birthday while lying in my bunk listening to the C141 Starlifter airplanes taking off from nearby McChord Airfield.

Graduation was a special time for us; Barney and I were close enough to have family there as we paraded around in our dress uniform for the final ceremony, proud of what we had done. I marched across that drill field as my family watched from the nearby bleachers, my chest swelled with pride. I had not realized it, but the Army had saved my life.

Finishing basic training was a major accomplishment in my life and I was looking forward to what I could do in the Army. I knew there would be challenges ahead. We took a much-needed break with two weeks off in between basic and tank training and we went home in our fancy dress uniforms and with some money in our pockets. By now everybody was talking about Vietnam, so it was then I started reading the news and watching television coverage. Barney and I took this time to relax and spend some time with family and then we were off again. We were shipped to Fort Knox in central Kentucky, home to the bullion depository where the U.S. gold reserves are stored. It was there that reality of Vietnam began to sink in.

Though the atmosphere at tank training was stern, we realized immediately it was more relaxed and focused than basic training had been. We still had drill sergeants, but we had more freedoms—including access to alcohol. We were quick to learn a pass was a good thing, and as often as we could we would go in groups to Louisville and do what all soldiers did: party and search for girls, or visit the Louisville USO where the staff was friendly and the atmosphere was inviting. During one trip to Louisville a dozen or so of us stayed the night in one hotel room because we couldn't afford to stay anywhere else. It wasn't until we returned that we learned one of the guys had the measles, although neither Barney nor I ever contracted them.

Just like at Fort Lewis, drill sergeants took us through our training, while other instructors taught us the finer points of the M48 medium tank. Most were experienced tank crewmembers, but at the time the Army was increasing the pace of training and I remember the cadre churning us through the course. During this time training and education began to become more important to me; I realized the tasks being taught could mean the difference between life and death. But the reality was that you mastered what you were doing today, and then tomorrow you did a brain dump and began to learn the next steps and procedures. I felt there had to be a better way to teach young adults to learn and retain knowledge. In the end, I just had to hope we remembered the important parts when the time was right.

We did not finish with our platoon. While our classmates would graduate and join units heading to Vietnam, Barney and I had a date with the United States Army Airborne School. We left Kentucky early for Fort Benning, Georgia, where we were a couple of new privates standing alongside 411 other soldiers, mostly sergeants and lieutenants, all reporting for Airborne training. We started our first week, Ground Week, like every other "Airborne," which would be our name until graduation; every trainer was called "Sergeant Airborne." Our instructors each wore black hats with the silver wings of a Jumpmaster, and we were to address them as Sergeant Airborne, as in "Yes, Sergeant Airborne" and "Moving, Sergeant Airborne."

School was similar all over the Army. We started our days at 0500 with physical training—running and exercises—and we usually ended up in a gravel pit doing "gravel drills." These are exercises in which you lie on either your front side or your back, or stay upright running in place. Your instructor is continuously and repetitively trying to get you to cycle through all three of the positions, one right after the other, while barking out commands like "Front!" "Back!" "Go!" Dog tired and weary, we would then move in formation to training where we would jump out of mock airplanes while learning how to fall properly. One of the important steps to master before moving to the Tower Phase was the parachute landing fall, a body position that included such positions as knees together and chin tucked to your chest.

As my training progressed I continued to gain confidence with every challenge. In going from a high school student to completing Army boot camp, advanced training, and now Airborne School, I was challenging myself and achieving new goals, which I continually adjusted. I figured there was no second place and I was not going to let myself fail. Whether it was five more push-ups or just one more mile, I knew I could make it to the finish line if I just pushed myself. I always told myself that I should try something once, and airborne training was no different. I worried about injuries or falls, but I figured I would deal with it if it were to happen.

We were always running and we were not to ever fall out. One day in Tower Week our "stick" (the name for a group of parachutists jumping from the same exit door of an aircraft on the same drop zone) was finishing the day's training and we were to join the rest of the students heading back when Sergeant Airborne let them move out ahead of us. Our cadre decided we would sprint to the backs of the other formations and then run circles around the other sticks, one at a time. We would sprint up to a formation, circle them, and then sprint ahead to the next group. This was no "airborne shuffle."

Ours was the only group doing this and we were all tired from the days training, and one of our classmates began to falter. I was one of the two on his sides and the other soldier and I reached out and locked arms with him to pull him along with us. Sergeant Airborne saw what we were doing and threatened that if we didn't let him go now he would drop us from the course. We let go as we watched him fall further behind; we assumed the cadre intercepted him and "washed" him out. We never saw him again.

Jump week had us in the C119 "Flying Boxcar," an airplane many would rather leave than stay inside. Though I had paid attention through all my training I was a little nervous, which surprised me because I thought I would have been more afraid. I was just as excited as scared to be going through it. I knew soldiers break legs or get hurt in other ways, but I was not in any hurry to fail out of jump school for anything—I knew I just had to get through this final week. For my first jump, they loaded us on the plane and we flew to our proper altitude. Then the Jumpmaster called our stick forward. The next thing I knew I was out of the plane, counting "one-thousand, two-thousand, three-thousand, four-thousand." Before I even noticed I felt the pull of the chute and I was under the canopy. It wasn't until my third jump that I tried opening my eyes; it was only then that I was starting to feel better and more confident in myself and my training. On my fifth jump, I was qualified to wear the silver jump wings of a paratrooper, and so was my pal Barney. We knew we had completed a tough course, but it was time to move on to our next challenge.

Of the 411 soldiers who signed in to that airborne class with us and of those who eventually graduated in May 1967, seven of us shipped out to Vietnam. As for Barney and me, we were going to be "Sky Soldiers" of the 173rd Airborne Brigade. It wasn't until after I arrived at that unit's base camp in country that I learned that was not going to happen for me; I was to be reassigned to the 1st Infantry Division. I sadly said my goodbyes to my pal Barney, not even considering that I would never see him again.

Understanding Tilley

As iron sharpens iron, so one person sharpens another.
—Proverbs 27:17

Service in the United States Armed Forces is a selfless act that few of our countrymen choose to perform, much less make a career as a professional soldier. I never set out to be a soldier for life but learned through my trials and tribulations that there was nothing else I would rather do. Being a soldier, marine, sailor, airman, or coast guardsman is a calling that over 3.5 million people currently answer among the active, guard, and reserve forces; the total active Army personnel strength is under 500,000 today, and getting smaller. These men and women serve as the vanguard that defends a nation of over 300 million people, and are the people I have come to know and love as brother and sister.

The military lifestyle and war, and the people who serve them, has been the subject of countless hours of study, and it changes the lives of the people who serve. Like many of my comrades, the experiences that were uniquely mine helped shaped me, as well as influence the relationships formed by those with whom I served. As a young soldier in a complicated period for America I was not in the best position to evaluate the political, economic, military, or societal implications of the Vietnam War. I was young and inexperienced in worldly matters, just a kid looking for adventure.

As Private Tilley, my most important job was to carry out orders. I watched what I was supposed to do, I learned from those around me, and I listened to my sergeants. I soon began to understand the roles and responsibilities of a basic soldier.

Throughout my training and my eventual deployment to Vietnam I just assumed that if I did those things I would be okay. There were over 211,000 U.S. service members killed or wounded in that conflict and surely many of them listened to their sergeants as well; it was up to me to learn all that I could to prepare myself for the unknown.

I had a very specific job that included a series of individual tasks that I was required to perform, and it was my number-one priority to do that in the hope that I would keep myself and my fellow soldiers alive. The lessons taught to me by the people I came in contact during my introductory training in the United States Army was instrumental in setting the foundation for my career. Any success I was to have in the military came during those most impressionable periods of initial entry training and jump school, and set the path for me to become the person I am today.

[2]

From 18 to 55

Troop A was without question the best, most proficient unit with which I ever served. A "perfect storm" of events brought together a unique collection of officers and NCOs, and many of us had served together in Germany and had learned our trade there. We all were high on the learning curve and needed only to adapt to the Vietnam environment. Serving at that time and place was a professional pleasure. Prepared and Loyal!

— Col. Ben Fegan, U.S. Army, Retired
former Commander, Troop A, 1st Battalion,
4th Cavalry Regiment

April 13, 1967

Arriving in Vietnam was both exciting and scary. Barney and I were just coming off thirty days' leave and we were put on a contracted airplane filled with GIs at Oakland Army Base in California. It was the self-declared "Gateway to the Vietnam War," and from where we embarked on a flight that with connections took more than twenty hours to arrive in Saigon. Weary from travel, our planeload of fresh-faced soldiers shuffled off to learn which units we were to be assigned to. Until we knew that information, all we could do was rest up at the "repo depo" (reception station) until somebody would call out our names in one of the seemingly endless formations.

With nothing to do, Barney and I headed over to the barracks. When we looked inside we saw that there were people and gear scattered everywhere among a series of stripped bunk beds consisting of nothing but a frame and exposed springs. Someone motioned for us to go draw a mattress but I was too tired to deal with it; I just picked out an empty rack, threw my duffel bag on the springs, and then climbed on top of the bunk and crashed. Others were more adventurous and toured the base; Bien Hoa Air Base was a huge base near Long Bin run by the Air Force, with the Army and other branches having a lesser presence. I knew tomorrow that we would soon be on our way so I wanted to sleep while I could.

At some time in the middle of the night I woke up to yelling and a scuffle at a nearby bunk. A couple of guys had gone out and discovered where they could get booze, and were now apparently in a drunken brawl over a mattress. The majority of those in the room had come in on the plane together and many were trying to sleep, but the lights came on and people in the room shouted at them to settle down until someone eventually pulled them apart and poured them into a rack. That first night in country was a restless one, the first of many bewildering sights and experiences. The next day, after yet another formation, a sergeant finally called out our names: Barney and I were to be assigned to the 173rd Airborne Brigade and were sent to their reception station for further instructions.

The 173rd was a historic unit with its roots in World War I. Due to its proximity to Vietnam from its base in Okinawa, it had the distinction of being the Army's first ground combat unit committed to the war. Early in 1967 the 173rd had made the only combat jump by a unit for the entire war and the men of that unit had been bloodied. The brigade had been in combat for over two years by then and much of their bravado had faded as a truckload of replacements like Barney and I filtered in—many of us filling in the ranks and taking our places in these units. There was mass confusion as we arrived, with people coming and going. New arrivals and those returning home were intermingled. We were just trying to be inconspicuous and make sure we took care of ourselves and kept track of our gear as we waited for someone to give us our next order. A soldier at the replacement center called me over, telling me that the nearby 1st Infantry Division had suffered some heavy losses and they were redirecting me to a place called Di An (pronounced Zeon). I would be going without Barney.

By now Barney and I had formed a bond that had taken us from our circle of hometown friends to the challenges of Army life. Through basic and advanced training, along with parachute school and the times in between, Barney and I had leaned on one another. Now I was going to continue this journey without him. With handshakes and good-natured ribbing, he went on and joined the Sky Soldiers, and I was loaded into a truck bound for the 1st Division replacement center.

The trucks were a regular method of moving people, with the standard 2.5-ton truck referred to as a "deuce-and-a-half." It was a three-axle, six-wheel transport vehicle that was not designed for frontline operations. Yet the nature of that war meant there were no declared front lines; the entire country was inherently risky, though some places were much more dangerous than others. I was told to load my gear in the back of the truck and I and a few other guys were issued M14 rifles. I asked about bullets and the sergeant told me that I would "get them when I get to my unit." The driver motioned me to load up, and off we went. I found myself sitting in the back of the truck on wooden bench seats, protected from the sun—but not from enemy fire—by a rolled-up canvas tarp that helped keep in the stifling heat. I just knew if we got into the shit on that ride that I was going to be dead meat.

The Big Red One, as the division was known, had major base camps at Di An, Phu Loi, Lai Khe, and Phuoc Vinh. Di An was the division's main base camp. There they assigned me a cot in a tent for replacements and we began to in-process the division by filling out forms and signing for gear. I attended a weeklong orientation and training program reviewing many of the tactics for jungle fighting, like dealing with booby traps, reading signals when entering a village, and understanding the capabilities and limitations of tanks in Vietnam. The training program was valuable to me and it was taught by skilled professionals who were well versed in the strengths, weaknesses, and tactics of the enemy. The training was designed to help fill in the information gaps in the "how-to" of jungle warfare to supplement what we had already been exposed to in stateside training centers. The information was meant to help keep us alive so I paid close attention to everything they told me. It became another example of where training and education helped me gain confidence in myself and my leaders.

After I completed my orientation, it was time for me to report to my unit. I was sent to Phu Loi where I was to be assigned to Troop A of the 1st Squadron, 4th Cavalry Regiment. My platoon, the 2nd Platoon of Alpha Troop, was cross-attached to an infantry battalion in our sector; one of their infantry platoons was cross-attached to our Troop. The platoon was already in the field and they were expecting me. I eventually met up with my platoon sergeant, Sgt. 1st Class Daniel DeButts, who then assigned me to the crew of an

ACAV. He told me I was going to be an "M60 AG," or the M60 machine gun assistant gunner.

By tradition, and as a means of esprit de corps, military units often adopt or are given nicknames that are based on events, gallantry, or legends. My squadron's nickname was "Dragoon" and the commander was known as "Dragoon 6," with the number six designating someone in a command position and making it easier to identify him in radio communication. And just like a tail number on a plane, a vehicle "bumper number" can tell you a bit about the role or purpose of a military vehicle, the unit it is assigned to, and the roles of the people it carries. Alpha Troop was "Hardcore," and our commander, at that time Capt. Ben Fegan, went by the call sign "Dragoon Alpha 6." Our platoon leader, 1st Lt. Smith, was "Dragoon Alpha 26" and his ACAV was numbered A26. The number 2 in 26 signified 2nd Platoon.

After the July 11, 1967 attack, I was assigned as a loader for now-Platoon Sergeant Ahsbahs' tank, A25. The number 5 in 25 signified the senior noncommissioned officer of 2nd Platoon. My new "home" was not cushy: The inside of the belly of a tank was not necessarily designed for comfort and I could never seem to find a good place to position myself in the M48. So, you could imagine my excitement when a few days later I would be moved to the driver's seat and get a compartment all to myself. Unfortunately, it was through the loss of DeButts and crew that this cavalryman earned his spurs as a tank driver in combat.

Soldiers have been nicknaming equipment like planes, tanks, and bombs for generations, and our platoon was no different. Whether it was painted on or in chalk lettering, nicknames or challenges allowed soldiers to take a bit more pride in themselves and their units. We sometimes pushed the boundaries of military customs and courtesies in picking a name, which hardly seemed a concern in places like this. Our vehicle names had to start with the letter A because we were in A Troop. Our vehicle was named *Antibiotic*, which was lovingly hand painted on both sides of the turret for all to see, and that tank was to be home for the remainder of my time in Vietnam.

The penetrator of a rocket-propelled grenade like the RPG-7 leaves a surprisingly small hole when it pierces the hull of a tank, but it is the melting of the hull after it passes through steel that creates molten fragments that cause the most damage. A shaped-charge penetrator does not cleanly pass through an armored vehicle, but sends flesh-tearing fragments throughout the compartment killing and maiming the men inside. It created an ugly scene, as our unit discovered after the attack: Captain Fegan got into a yelling match with the commander of the Division Support Command when the full colonel told him that he not only had to keep DeButts's tank following the latter's death, but that the men of A Troop were going to recover the remains of our fallen comrades. Fegan was livid and refused, and demanded that Graves Registration troops complete the work. The DISCOM Commander finally relented and our platoon was spared the added insult of recovering our men, but no cleaning in the world was going to ever remove the memories of those we lost. The smell of death never left tank A25.

Later when we were moving our gear over to A25 and replacing the expended ammunition, I reached down to grab one of the ammunition boxes stored inside the turret storage bins and saw what appeared to be some remains missed by the recovery crew. It was a section of the hand of one of my platoon mates, Pvt. 1st Class Lewis F. Jenkins. I reached down and gently collected three severed fingers and found a small box to place them in. Unsure of what else to do, I found a bit of ground near the tank and dug a hole and buried the remains. I said a prayer over them for Jenkins and the other men lost, and I covered the box in dirt in what seemed to me like a proper burial.

It was soon after that when I became Ahsbahs' tank driver permanently. Ahsbahs was the first noncommissioned officer that I could say I knew as a person, and someone I came to deeply respect. A German citizen and thus not subject to the draft, he served in the United States Army as a matter of choice and had a unique perspective about the war. A year earlier U.S. Navy pilot Lt. j.g. Dieter Dengler, another native of Germany, had been shot down and held captive by the North Vietnamese for four months, undergoing torture before finally making his escape. After learning of this, Ahsbahs approached Fegan and explained that he felt like he needed to be sent home so he wouldn't suffer a similar fate. After Fegan listened to his story, he calmly told Ahsbahs he wasn't going to let that happen to him, which seemed to satisfy Ahsbahs. He returned to his duties. Not only was he loyal to those around him, he was loyal to those he served.

If I ever knew much of what we were up to at the time, I had long forgotten the objective and purpose of many of our missions and functions. I wore private first class stripes and I was just a tank driver who listened to his sergeant. I did the best I could to keep my tank rolling. When it was time, day or night, I would get on the tank and go where I was told. Other days were spent checking my equipment: are the oils levels full, are the rotating tracks tension-adjusted properly, is it properly lubed? Ahsbahs had his job to do and I wasn't too much privy to it; my job was to keep the tank rolling and get us to where directed as quickly and as safely as I could, and I did that. I loved nothing more than the exhilaration of leading the formation as we would go out on missions. I loved to lead the pack.

Soon after my arrival in country I had been given a bible by some long-forgotten soul, possibly a chaplain or one of the volunteers who gave so much to be among the GIs. I remember carrying it back to my tank and throwing it in an old ammunition container that I had begun to use to hold some of my personal effects, and I forgot about it. A few months later I remember finding it while retrieving something and I felt inclined to open it up. I was shocked when the first page that I opened it to had what appeared to be a spot of blood on it.

When I first received the bible, it was brand-new so I scanned the other pages and saw that none of them had a similar spot and noticed there was no red ink anywhere in the bible. To me this was a sign of divine protection, so I put it back in the ammo can and kept it stored in the driver's compartment near me. Occasionally I would pull it out and read passages, but just seeing it or the ammo can that held it gave me a sense of comfort. After a while it began to feel like my good-luck charm, especially those times after we escaped another attack or roadside mine unscathed. Over time that would be one of the things I checked before we moved out or left the firebase.

My first couple of months with the 1/4 Cav. were a blur as I adjusted to the unit's missions and rhythms. Though I was one of the new guys, I soon saw a familiar face: one of my instructors from Fort Knox was there with me in Alpha Troop. We searched for roadside mines on the supply routes and conducted search-and-destroy missions. The roadsides were often mined, so as we would "sweep" we would travel dead-center of the width of the road, forcing locals over onto the shoulder. Oftentimes we would run a sweep on a portion of the route, then lie in wait to ambush anyone trying to rig up explosives. At the end of a mission we would sweep the routes to our next destination. It was during this time that my AIT instructor was killed and I came to a realization of the finality of war.

It was three weeks after I arrived when he was killed during the battle along "Thunder Road," the nickname given to Highway 13. Along its path was the village of Quon Loi. The Michelin Tire Company had constructed a rubber plantation many years ago alongside the highway and it was now abandoned. The highway was closed to traffic, but during harvest time we would sometimes reopen the highway to allow for resupply and harvesting. Quon Loi was built on red clay that would get everywhere and stick when it was wet, or turn into a fine red power when it was dry. The base camp was in the middle of the plantation in a building we called the "Frenchman's House," which was off-limits to U.S. military personnel. It was flanked by abandoned colonial-style buildings and its own French oasis, a once-lavish swimming pool. It was here during the harvest season that our platoon was repeatedly attacked and where we lost both our platoon leader and platoon sergeant.

It wasn't until then that I really experienced the tragedy of war—this fellow was someone I had learned from and trained with. The confidence I gained up to this point was fading as I thought of the hopelessness of my situation. I felt that if the man who helped train and prepare me for combat could die, and he was much more experienced and better prepared, then how would I ever have a chance? The thought of that just scared the hell out of me. It was worse knowing that he did everything right and did exactly what one was expected to do in those circumstances, yet he was a victim of fate. I had been told throughout my training of the soldier's role, that at some point we might have to lay down our lives in performing our duties. I now knew clearly just what that meant.

It wasn't just the danger of the enemy we were facing; there were other hazards that were just as perilous. The ACAV gunners would sit exposed on top of the vehicles on boxes of C-rations during these missions because there was no platform, and standing in the personnel hatch did not afford them a clear view. It was during a turning maneuver while busting brush that one of the guys fell off the ACAV to the ground and broke his back. During a major battle as part of a search-and-destroy mission we were attempting to enter a textile plant when one of the ACAVs drove down a small cliff. The crew was banged up, so we hightailed it out to find level ground and a better route to break through; eventually an ACAV rammed through a wall and got inside the plant. What we didn't see were the Vietcong troops waiting in a nearby tower. They fired and hit the ACAV with an RPG. The crew ran like hell and jumped on another vehicle, but the platoon leader did not want to leave the ACAV.

We regrouped and they devised a plan in which my tank would go back in with main gun firing, and two ACAVs would follow. One of them would take up a position to engage the tower and the other would hook a tow rope to the blown-up ACAV and tow it out. Well, that was the plan.

In reality, our tank made it through and the two ACAVs did not. The next thing we knew we were out in the open and alone firing our guns. Since we were already there and the VC were disorganized, we changed the plan. It seemed like they weren't expecting us, so while they were busy dodging our rounds we went ahead and hooked up to the ACAV ourselves and dragged it out. Once we got it back to the platoon assembly area, the driver went in and cranked it up. We came to find out that we could have driven it out on its own.

Events on the battlefield can be horrific and grisly, but at the conclusion soldiers mop up and move on to the next task. As comrades are evacuated from the battlefield because of injury or death, many are faced with a lifetime of care and rehabilitation. Meanwhile the unit just presses on, often losing sight of the individuals who were most affected by the incidents. Many seemed to compartmentalize these feelings to function, but eventually thoughts and reminders might quickly take them back to those moments in a rush of emotions and fear. It is the lingering result of combat that many soldiers experience.

Understanding Tilley

Never in the field of human conflict was so much owed by so many to so few.
—Winston Churchill

Loyalty and trust was built between Fegan and Ahsbahs, which was displayed by Ahsbahs in his relationship with his crew. During my first major attack in Vietnam, Ahsbahs showed the example of a cool and collected leader during a life-threatening event that led me to see him as a man of strength and character. I knew that I could trust him because of his behaviors and actions, and as a leader I would often emulate his style. As a young soldier, I didn't always understand the mission or the why or how of what we were doing. But I knew my sergeant was counting on me, and I didn't want to let him down.

The body's reaction to life-and-death situations like the type faced in a war zone can be debilitating; experts refer to it as a "fight or flight" reaction. Sometimes the response may not even come to light until soldiers return, even months and years later. Soldiers and leaders should know the signs of stress, and monitor themselves and others after being exposed to intense or traumatic events. And don't assume that because you are coping that those around you should be able to as well. The world is a dangerous place and war zone–like stressors can happen most anywhere in this contemporary environment—as in the case of 9/11 in New York and the Pentagon or the rampages at supposed "safe havens," like Fort Hood, Texas or the Chattanooga, Tennessee, reserve center.

Soldiers that suffer from the effects of the body's response to combat should seek advice and counsel from a trusted person, especially if those responses are interfering with their performance or quality of life. There are many skilled professionals that may be able to help you or your soldiers get the assistance needed. If you are unsure about professional help you may want to talk to a peer, mentor, or family member, because they may help you see yourself better than you can. And always be on alert for signs of stress in your soldiers, peers, leaders, and even our Soldier for Life veterans and retirees.

Leaders have worked hard to erase the perceived stigma of seeking help as a sign of weakness, but it is tough to change a culture, especially one as "macho" or "HOOAH" as the Army. Some of the most stubborn to recognize and take action after identifying signs and symptoms of combat stress in themselves are leaders; no soldier is immune. Making self-assessments, having a trusted family member or battle buddy to help you monitor yourself, and understanding and using coping skills provided by mental health experts are sure ways to stay connected to where you are mentally. Be open to advice and even possible criticism of your personality and attitude, and be sensitive to warning signs, you are too important not to.

[3]

Tet '68

As darkness descended over the 100 troopers of Troop A, 1st Squadron, 4th Cavalry north of Saigon on January 30, 1968, none of them realized that in less than 24 hours they would be part of the force protecting Saigon during the 1968 Tet Offensive. Jack Tilley and his fellow troopers had trained to be jungle warriors and were now used for an urban fight. They were able to do that because of leadership, leadership at all levels—to include each trooper who inspired those troopers around him. Tet taught Tilley and his fellow troopers what they were made of, lessons of life that no organization could be successful without leadership.

—Lt. Col. Fred W. Shirley, U.S. Army Retired
former commander, Troop A, 1st Battalion,
4th Cavalry Regiment

January 31, 1968, 0200hrs

The first month of 1968 was drawing to a close and I had less than three left in country. I couldn't wait to get back home. We were under a cease-fire because of the Vietnamese New Year—Tet—but we remained on high alert, and on this night, somebody was in a damn hurry. Our tanks and ACAVs were quickly lined up and we were rushed off our base camp to establish a nighttime defensive position along another god-forsaken stretch of Highway 13. The only sounds I heard while our preparation was underway were those made through the intercom between the tank commander, the loader, and myself. After a while you get used to the sounds of background radios and the discussion of operations, and I no longer paid them much mind. I hardly ever seemed to know what was happening next, which over time really begins to take its toll.

Until that night we had been running mounted security patrols within our operation area, and this seemed just like another exercise of "hurry up and wait." We had been running patrols during the day, after which we would return to our positions at night to rest up and get ready for the next. When we were back at camp and in between missions, we could relax some, though it was never safe anywhere. We were mostly young men; we all took part in the typical grab-ass that boredom causes. But once we were outside the wire we took our jobs seriously. When parked along the road, even when in tanks or lightly armored personnel carriers, we were exposed to the enemy. Losing our edge or being complacent could often mean the difference between living and dying. I served alongside great men who were sent abroad by our nation to do its bidding, but under those conditions it was each other who we were fighting for. Small-unit leadership was the most fundamental trait that kept us going, and what I attribute my survival to—that, and a whole lot of luck and good fortune.

Word came down that the cease-fire had been lifted and we were heading out. By now it was well beyond midnight on a winter's night. In the jungle things always looked different at night. Shadows danced and your eyes played tricks on you. Sounds, moonlight, or light aids often masked reality on the ground. On some evenings, you couldn't even see your hand in front of your face, while on others the moon would light up the vegetation and make it appear as if there were ghosts walking among the trees.

That evening the perils of operating at night quickly became apparent. Maybe it was due to the speed at which we left, or maybe updates hadn't reached them, but unbeknown to us a pair of American helicopter gunships spotted our position from a distance and took an interest in us. The crews got it in their minds that we had no business being where we were and that we were not friendlies, so they attacked our formation with rockets. We all just froze in place until the shooting stopped, and then hauled ass back to our tanks. It was only after some tense moments on the radio that they were called off. Luckily no one was hurt or killed.

After that we knew it was time to get the hell out of there. We formed up with the rest of our squadron, which meant that something big must be going on. The whole platoon was unsettled; we hadn't cleared the roads that day and so we didn't know what lay ahead. As soon as the sun came up on January 31 we were out of there. Our platoon was ordered to move out quickly in the direction of Saigon, destination unknown. The war's largest military operation to date, Tet 1968, was now underway.

We headed out going cross-country, which slowed progress but was less risky than the paved roads. Everyone realized the seriousness of the situation when at one point our division commander came on our command radio frequency to tell us to hurry the hell up and get on the highway. Though I usually tried to lead the platoon movements every chance I got, I was fine when this time we were the second vehicle. The lead tank had barely turned onto the highway when it hit a pressure-detonated mine that blew off the tank treads. The tank was disabled but there was no time to stop and help. We pressed on.

My tank took the point and we moved forward. I grabbed my seldom-used flak vest and put in on my seat and sat on it. I figured if I hit a mine that little bit of protection might keep the hull-mounted escape hatch below from being blown clean through my ass. On the uncleared roads we soon encountered roadblocks, but the burning piles of debris and tires were no match for our armored column. I hit cars and the burning debris piles straight-on: I would lean into the tank and bowl over the abandoned vehicles the enemy was using to try to channel our column to the route he wanted us to drive, which was likely mined. After several hours, we made it to Highway 316 and awaited orders, and I took the time to check out my tank. I saw that it was leaking oil in three places. Word got back to us that the division staff was amazed at how far we had gone.

We were unaware of the magnitude of the coordinated and simultaneous attacks on the major U.S. bases and Republic of Vietnam troop concentrations that were occurring across Vietnam. It wasn't until we crossed over the Newport Bridge, a major artery leading into Saigon, that we began to understand the scale of what was happening. Vietcong guerrillas repeatedly attacked the capital city from all directions using upwards of thirty-five battalions. The Presidential Palace, the U.S. Embassy, and Tan Son Nhut Air Base were believed to be high-priority targets for the VC, and our mission was to provide relief to the beleaguered air base.

I topped off the tank's oil levels and we headed out towards Tan Son Nhut. We were urged forward because the base was still under attack and was at risk to fall. We had spent the better part of our time in and among the jungles along dry rice paddies, and were unaccustomed to improved road surfaces and city fighting. Our tactics had to change; it was not roadside bombs that were the main threats, but snipers and small-arms fire. We hunkered down in our vehicles with our hatches closed as we moved through the city. The scene in Saigon was unreal: There were dead bodies, smoke, fires, and destruction all around. Our maneuvering room was restricted and we could not follow our usual tactic of recon by fire, and we had to take out snipers on rooftops and in windows using small, dismounted teams. The VC used sappers who infiltrated many key areas of the city, and the civilian and military casualties were mounting. Our battalion commander, Lt. Col. John Siegel, had his helicopter shot down by enemy fire, and it was only through the pilot's skill that the crippled bird was able to safely land. The carnage was all around us, and as we neared the base we saw bodies strewn haphazardly.

Because of the lunar New Year much of the Vietnamese Air Force was on leave. What remained for security at the air base by the time we arrived was a force of Air Force security police, the quick-reaction forces of a Signal Battalion, and fellow cavalrymen from 3rd Squadron, 4th Cavalry Regiment, who did much of the fighting. When we pulled up there were signs of a heavy battle: dead Vietnamese sappers, were hung up in the wire surrounding the base. They had been killed while trying to breach the perimeter.

Troop C of 3/4 Cav. had been alerted to the VC offensive the same morning as we had, they had left before first light on the 31st with orders to relieve the base security. It was approaching dusk by the time we arrived and much of the fighting was done, with Troop C mopping up. The 3/4 Cav. commander, Lt. Col. (later Gen.) Glenn K. Otis, was controlling much of the Army response at Tan Son Nhut. Our troop was tied in to the 3/4 Cav. defenses at the west end of the runway as we settled in for whatever was to happen.

Though the fiercest fighting had subsided, we were not done. The Air Force had pilots living off-base in temporary

Bachelor Officer Quarters in the nearby village, and we were given the mission of finding and retrieving the officers. We found the first building without too much trouble and our platoon was left to secure the site while the rest of the troop went out for the others. Those pilots were pretty happy to see the Army show up with tanks and personnel carriers to take them to the relative safety of the base, but instead we stayed with them until we were given the signal we could return. The next morning, we were ordered back with our charges in tow. A Troop was put under the operational control of Otis and for the rest of the day we resupplied our ammo and performed some much-needed maintenance on our vehicles.

It had been over thirty-six hours since we left Phu Loi, and my seemingly endless supply of adrenaline was running low. I remember sitting down and eating a hot meal—thanks to 3/4 Cav.—with what must have been hundreds of dead, swollen bodies just lying around and I wasn't even phased by it. I knew they were there but it was like I could not see them. Many were killed by napalm and were burned alive; the sights and smells were something that no person would want to experience. It was such a surreal sight, and at the time I gave it so little thought that it seemed like an out-of-body experience. It was not until after the fight that the thoughts and images of that moment began to linger, and I realized the events of those days are not what a civilized person would expect to experience in his or her lifetime. The seeming lack of empathy for human life is sometimes tough to reconcile for those who have never had the experience of war, and the events of Tet are forever etched upon my brain.

It wasn't until the next day that we were to go out on our next operation, a reconnaissance in force with one of the infantry battalions from the 25th Infantry Division and with our temporary higher headquarters, the 3/4 Cav. The infantry was to do a detailed search of a village called Ap Dong while the cavalry would provide security. Evidently the VC battalion that holed up there wasn't expecting this large a force, so when we descended on them they headed for the hills and 2nd Platoon was sent to head them off before they could escape. Our lead tank came under attack but barreled its way through the enemy position trying to cut off the escaping VC troops. Meanwhile other parts of the troop were coming under fire, and 1st Sergeant Frank Kather was seriously burned when he and the crew of the personnel carrier in which he was riding were hit with an antitank round. Of the five men, Kather was the most seriously injured.

A platoon had taken up a position to bring fire upon the enemy forces, but now it was the target of heavy fire from the village. Our platoon was called to provide them some relief and the lead tank began targeting the houses with its main gun. These stucco-style homes offered no protection from our rounds; after putting rounds into about five of the buildings, the guns were silenced. It was during this fight that our platoon leader, Lt. John Hammonds, was injured and lost sight in one of his eyes. He, 1st Sgt. Kather, and three others from the first sergeant's ACAV had to be medically evacuated. The track they were on was deemed a combat loss and had to be destroyed by a thermite grenade.

For the next couple of days, we assisted the 3/4 Cav. by conducting sweeps, establishing defensive positions, and handling other mop-up operations. After a week of supporting a number of different units we were sent back through Saigon to a water filtration plant where we would rejoin the fighting with the 1st Infantry Division. Troop A was now under the operational control of the 2nd Brigade and for the next two months we would operate with different battalions of that brigade, protecting the water plant and conducting route security along Highway 316.

Like all soldiers in "The 'Nam" the two dates I knew best were the date I arrived in country and the date I was scheduled to leave, the latter being June 1968. After Tet, I was promoted to Specialist 5 while mop-up operations in Saigon and the surrounding area continued, that went on until mid-February. By all official accounts Tet 1968 continued to the end of March.

As I continued about in my daily activities, the reality of the finality of war was about to slap me again right in my face. I was summoned back to battalion where I learned that my hometown buddy Barney was killed in battle and I was being requested by his family to escort his remains home. I would later learn that Pvt. 1st Class Prentis Barney Boykin Jr. and seven of his comrades of Company D (Airborne), 16th Armor, 173rd Airborne Brigade were killed in an attack on March 4, 1968, only a few weeks before we were scheduled to go home.

Understanding Tilley

"Cry 'Havoc!', and let slip the dogs of war."

—William Shakespeare,
Julius Caesar

What mattered most to my leaders was that I was trained and equipped to do what they asked of me, and that I followed the orders of those leaders appointed over me. As the Soldier Creed states "*I am disciplined, physically and mentally tough, trained and proficient in my warrior tasks and drills.*" A cohesive military unit is not like a sports team where if you lose you come back another day to play. In our profession, if you are ill prepared for combat you lose—which could mean loss of life. Every soldier is a member of an integral team, whether at the crew, team, squad, or platoon level, and as such we have to rely on one another to do our respective parts. I may or may not have been the best-informed soldier on the battlefield, but I had confidence in my abilities, trust in my leaders, and the belief that we would be able to succeed. A unit's success is measured by the sum of its parts and for that series of events it was clearly the people and their abilities that made the difference to the overall outcome to our mission.

How do you prepare to lose a brother-in-arms? Today the Army puts a lot of effort in building resiliency in its soldiers, helping develop skills to face and cope with such situations. I recognize that for many, Vietnam is generations away. But when a soldier is faced with violence and fear firsthand, and without the proper training in how to deal with the body's natural reaction to the stress of combat, it can significantly affect a soldier's emotional, physical, mental, and behavioral reactions. As an individual soldier, one must be self-aware enough to understand why you must adapt and work to become stronger mentally, physically, and emotionally. Leaders have the added responsibility to teach resiliency and to build trust among the soldiers within their care. Leaders coach and mentor by setting and enforcing standards, and in leading by example. This is a part of the DNA of the noncommissioned officer and we must each continue to learn and improve within this area.

Barney was lost in battle on March 4, 1968. In looking back 37-years at those events I am convinced that it takes a special person to be a soldier. You become a different person when you go to war and when you come back from war. You look at things differently. You understand life a lot differently and whether you know it or not at the time, it changes you in a lot of different ways. Tet wasn't my final battle, but it was key to understanding myself and how I handled adversity. It helped me prepare for the hardships ahead.

Through my numerous trips to hospitals and military trauma centers I was often reminded of the very visible toll combat can take on soldiers. What is harder to understand are the unseen injuries and effects of blast injuries, as well as the experiences soldiers have in dealing with the pain and of stress of combat. These will continue to be challenges for the individual soldier and veteran, and addressing these issues should remain a high priority for our nation.

[4]

Running from Yourself

The friendships I formed with Jack Tilley would help shape both of our careers and future assignments. I first met him after we were assigned to the same brigade at Fort Knox, Kentucky. What I always respected about Jack Tilley was that he always took care of his soldiers and family members and was always concerned about their career and welfare. Jack's record speaks for itself and all the great things he was able to accomplish in the best interest of the Army, Soldiers, and family members. Jack always did what was best for the Soldier.

—Cmd. Sgt. Maj. Gerald Utterback,
U.S. Army, Retired

March 5, 1968

I didn't leave Vietnam on that freedom bird to America like so many of my comrades. I instead escorted Barney home to Vancouver. After I was notified I went back to my squad to say my goodbyes and collect my things from my tank. Once there I reached for my .50-cal ammunition can where I kept my personal effects; I wanted to grab my talisman bible. As I rummaged around I saw it was gone, which was a sure sign to me that my luck had run out. I was briefed by the casualty assistance office before I left, and I was told that once Barney's remains were delivered that I would have to return to Vietnam to finish up my tour. But for now, I had the solemn task of caring for my friend.

I went wherever his casket went, never losing sight of it. I rendered honors every time it was moved, wondering about the fate that took him. I stayed with Barney until he was turned over to the funeral home, and I stayed and attended his service and paid my respects to his family and friends. His parents came to review his remains; the first person to open that casket was Barney's mom. I stood nearby while she looked at him, and I was sobbing and crying along with them. Vietnam had been such an influence on my young life, and at just barely twenty years old I was already putting a significant chapter of that life behind me. I spent many years pushing those memories to the furthest reaches of my mind, or so I thought. Little did I know that future events could cause them to come flooding back in an instant.

All these years later I am not sure if I can remember what happened that first month after I returned, but I do know I tried to drink all the beer I could get my hands on. It seemed like an eternity since I had left home and I felt like an old man now. I had aged and matured tremendously. War has a way of doing that to young people: you leave home a boy and return a man. All I wanted to do was turn off the switch from Vietnam and the bush. I needed a new pace and to establish a new rhythm. Now was a great time for me to take advantage of my saved leave time so I could relax and hang out with my friends. By this time Vietnam was a national conversation and everyone wanted to know about me and my tour, and mostly what it was like to fight in that war. This was a time for me to tell bullshit stories to my pals and puff out my chest some. I was playing it to the hilt; if they only understood how true my words were.

I had a pocket full of money and thought I needed a cool car, so I bought a flashy, red used MGB Roadster, a two-seat British sports car. Soon I was zipping up and down my old neighborhoods with the top down, enjoying the summer breeze and the fact that I was away from that god-awful place. But even in my fast sports car it wasn't easy to shake the ever-present memories of Vietnam. I found myself in a trance one day driving that MGB when I realized everyone on the highway was zooming past me. I looked down at my speedometer and I saw I was only traveling at about twenty-five miles per hour—roughly the same speed I would drive my tank in Vietnam. I had to snap myself out of the trance.

I don't think I ever heard at the time words like post-traumatic stress or other such labels, but the violence of war lingers on a soldier for life. It is how one copes that really matters, and we are just now teaching the importance of resiliency. Resiliency is an art to master, and doing so becomes more complicated when we expect young sergeants to teach others on how to deal with the after effects of war. At the time, I knew little of the distress war caused me through sights, sound, and smell, nor did I recognize the lasting effects. War had truly changed my life.

Soon I bid my friends and family farewell again, I was heading back to Fort Benning and this time I was to be permanent party. The Army decided with such a short amount of time remaining it was better just to assign me stateside. I was without a clue as to what challenge lay ahead for me. Besides the Airborne School, Benning was a major training installation conducting all types of initial military training, and it served as the home of the Infantry. It wasn't until after I arrived and during in-processing when a sergeant told me the Armor unit I was going to was full. Then he asked me, "Can you sing?" I laughed and told him, "No I can't sing, people leave the room when I sing." He just smiled and said, "Good, you're going to be a drill sergeant." And that was it.

It was 1968, the peak of the Vietnam conflict, and I was heading to Sand Hill to lead impressionable men during one of the most iconic phases of a military person's career. I would be in charge of the most important phase of their transition from civilian to soldier, and I couldn't wait. It was soon after my arrival that I was awarded the Bronze Star medal for valor for our unfortunate fate of being the sole defenders of the blown-up ACAV in Vietnam; the medal was later pinned on my chest far from the men who I had served alongside.

I knew what drill sergeants did. Drill Sergeant Lewis was an influential leader very early in my career, and the thought of following in his shoes was something that got me thinking. I was worried because I did not like to speak in public and the thought of getting up in front of people and talking bugged me. If someone introduced me in a crowd I could easily speak, but in a formal setting it was a challenge for me to talk professionally because it made me uncomfortable. So it was under these conditions that I was sent off to a basic training unit; unexpected news was that I was to be laterally promoted from Specialist 5 to a three-striper sergeant. For most of the next thirty-three years of my life I would be a noncommissioned officer.

The Army, in its infinite wisdom, did not just send vets like me straight to training. For the first couple of months after reporting to Fort Benning I was assigned to the Army Training Center as a drill sergeant in Company A, 10th Battalion, 2nd Training Brigade. At first, I served as a Drill Sergeant Candidate and "shadowed" the existing drill sergeants to watch and observe what they did. I used that time to prepare myself for what I knew would be a rigorous school and quizzed the drill sergeants on ways to be successful. There were no programs available to me at that time to help me prepare, but I knew that I wanted to take advantage of this new challenge to increase my limited skills. Such educational opportunities were few and far between and I wanted to make the best of it.

Drill Sergeant School was the toughest course I ever attended, not only because of my speaking fears, but because of the memorization requirements for learning all the drill movements and ceremonies. I was sent to Fort Jackson, South Carolina, one of the Army Training Centers that conducted this specialized training. Begun just a few years earlier in 1964 at the direction of Secretary of the Army Stephen Ailes, Drill Sergeant School was created to address the quality of Army Training Center noncommissioned officers.

Drill sergeant duty was tough, not just because of the high standards and training regime, but because of long working hours, the demanding nature of the work, and lack of free time for family concerns. Upon reporting in I realized this was going to be a mental challenge. As candidates, we were expected to master and teach a number of tasks that the newly inducted must go through to become a soldier. Though there were Committee Groups that conducted training to reduce the burden on the drill sergeants, much of the fundamental tasks a soldier must perform were taught or reinforced by their drill sergeant.

One of my first hurdles was to perfectly recite all the steps in teaching a trainee how to execute complex drill movements, as well as the various Army-approved exercises for physical training. We had to master all of the techniques for training enlistees in the basic fundamentals of soldiering, and we had to understand the behavior of groups. We had to study manuals and memorize each movement and be able to regurgitate it in perfect order, so it was not unusual to see my fellow classmates and I walking around reciting the various lessons in what appeared to be a loony bin of blathering idiots. To practice we would place ourselves in front of inanimate objects—my favorites were trees or floor polishers—while teaching them the finer points of the "seven steps of marching" or "squad drill." We did this by using rapid-fire delivery of phrases like "The next movement I will name, explain, demonstrate and you will conduct practical exercise on is the 'Right, Face.' 'Right, Face' is a two-part command, the preparatory command being 'Right' and command of execution being 'Face.' In its entirety it sounds like, 'Right, Face.'" By the first week I was mentally exhausted.

Going to Drill Sergeant School at that time in my short career was a perfect assignment to help me overcome a personal shortfall: my fear of talking in front of crowds. I was never going to develop my leadership style without a challenge like this to help me overcome adversity and meeting a weakness head-on, so I took the assignment in stride. Often you don't realize the importance of facing fears and conquering hurdles, but the challenge of Drill Sergeant School would be an important lesson for me, and one that came on the heels of a significant emotional event in my life. The discipline, attention to detail, and precision expected of my classmates and I smoothed out the rough spots I gained through my combat experience. This was to carry me onward for the next fifteen years, which would be the next time I attended a noncommissioned officer education course.

One time I was being graded on the physical training module and I drew one of the dreaded exercises, the "high jumper." The high jumper was not an extremely strenuous exercise in moderation, but some trainers would love to do fifty or one hundred repetitions. What made the high jumper so difficult was the simultaneous movements: You would jump from a crouching position while swinging your arms upward until they were completely vertical, and then move your head backward until you were looking up at the sky. While you were coming down you were to swing your arms backwards until they arrived at the starting position, about the same time you were landing and going back to a crouch position. Doing this at the normal cadence was difficult enough, but oftentimes it was a riot to watch an uncoordinated soldier out of sequence moving his arms up while his body was traveling downward, or so worried about the jump and the look that he forgot to move his arms.

I understood that exercise was the one that flubbed up a lot of candidates, and so I practiced over and over. When it was my turn to test, I marched right up to the front of the "squad" of other candidates, all of who were waiting their turn to test as well, and under the watchful eye of my drill sergeant instructor. I took over the squad and put them in the extended rectangular formation and began my commands:

Platoon, ATTENTION. AT EASE. The High Jumper is a four-count exercise done at a moderate cadence. At normal cadence, this exercise will look as follows. The High Jumper. Start position, MOVE. In cadence, EXERCISE.

Well, that is what I said in my mind; my mouth said something else that evidently wasn't good enough. I scored something like a 68 out of 100 and failed my first exam. I was devastated because I knew I studied my ass off and felt that if I couldn't pass that exercise after practicing that much then I wasn't going to be able to pass anything.

I was talking to my buddy and classmate S. Sgt. Harold Moore and just generally griping about my predicament. He listened to me for a bit and then he told me "I think you are studying too hard," and he convinced me to go to the NCO Club to blow off some steam. The two of us got rip-roaring drunk and we didn't roll back to the barracks until 0200 knowing we had reveille at 0400. I didn't even sleep in my bed that night; I just closed my eyes and lay on the floor for what felt like only a minute. I woke up two hours later and dragged my ass to the drill field, taking my licks for staying out late partying. When my time came around for my next exam, I was given a facing movement like Left Face, and this time I passed with flying colors and scored 100. I guess Drill Sergeant School wasn't as difficult as I made it out in my mind to be.

I was a typical middle-of-the-road soldier and a solid performer, but I continued to learn how to master my craft. Just like when I drove my tank in Vietnam, I was straight down the middle of the progression ladder. I never worried about things like when was I going to be promoted next; I simply kept my stuff straight and knew it would happen in time. My sergeants were not on my back and I was able to stay up with the rest of my peers and complete a tough course and beat another fear. At graduation, I was proud to don that "Smokey Bear" campaign hat and pin on the coveted drill sergeant badge. I did it with the help of those around me. It was there that I began to realize why nobody is successful by themselves.

For the last year of my initial enlistment I was to serve on drill sergeant status. I had yet to decide what to do until I reached that day. But for now, I was focused on my recruits and I was happy about what I was doing. I lived in the permanent party barracks about a half mile from my company. These were World War II–era buildings assembled as temporary spaces during the mass mobilization for that war, and they were still in widespread use. Like most, ours were elevated slightly above the ground on concrete cinder blocks. During this time, my attitudes and opinions about continued service were shifting, and the little things began to gnaw at me. I bought myself a television set for my room. Less than a week after I got it some bastard barracks thief stole it from me.

My final days in the Army grew closer and even though folks talked to me about staying in, being in the Army wasn't the hippest thing to do in 1968. I was doing okay as a soldier, preparing soldiers for likely combat. I was fine with that; I just hadn't made up my mind on what to do in the long term. I was doing a lot of drinking and partying, which made coping easier and kept me from having to deal with any troubles. But there was still one part that got under my skin, the one thing that bugged me the most: the piss-poor leadership of Capt. James G. Woodruff[2], my company commander.

Throughout my career I had met and worked with and for a number of interesting people, but in my young, impressionable mind Woodruff was the worst leader I had ever met. By then I had experienced nothing but professional Army leaders, those like DS Lewis at basic training and the many Sergeants Airborne at Airborne School, and combat leaders like Ahsbahs and the cadre of the Drill Sergeant School.

I am the kind of guy that can get along with just about anybody, but lives were at stake here. Woodruff's demeanor was abusive and downright terrible, and I began to get a chip

---

[2] Not his real name.

on my shoulder just working for this man. I had been lucky up to this point in the Army and hadn't had to deal with situations like this, but to me I felt like I had a trick up my sleeve to deal with his abuse: I would say to myself, "I'll show him" to help me get over the roughest spots. At the time, it was just an empty promise, but I knew I could make good on it.

I may have only been a young buck sergeant but I believe that even then I knew what right looked like. And in my opinion Woodruff was all wrong. We were charged with developing young men who would likely be in harm's way, and the things that he did and expected of us didn't make any damn sense. The other drill sergeants and I spoke about the issue but there was little we could do, he was the "old man" and it wasn't our responsibility to supervise him. Meanwhile I just sucked it up and dealt with it.

One of the leaders who countered Woodward for me and served as a true role model was my first sergeant, 1st Sergeant Elden Johnson. 1st Sgt. Johnson left a positive impression on many with whom he served. He was a hell of a guy who I learned a lot from. He helped me buy a car, a 1962 Ford Fairlane convertible, my MGB roadster had been long gone by now. He paid for it and I paid him back, which perfectly describes the kind of guy he was. I was cruising around Columbus, Georgia, instead of walking thanks to my first sergeant. He was a by-the-book NCO who led from the front in all that he did and he was a great role model. Though I was not sure where he stood on our commander and his actions, I not once ever saw him waiver in his loyalty to the command.

Promotion was not something that I thought a lot about. I was promoted to Pvt. 2nd Class out of AIT and then while in Vietnam I was advanced to Private 1st Class. I was promoted to Specialist 4 in Vietnam and then right before I left I was promoted to Specialist 5. It wasn't until I got back to Fort Benning that I became a "hard-stripe" sergeant. 1st Sgt. Johnson called me in to his office and told me I was going to a promotion board and that there were three other people up for staff sergeant as well. So, I studied as much as I could and prepared for the board; though it was my first-ever selection board I passed and was selected. I never had sought out promotions. I assumed that in the end if I did my job then promotion would eventually come.

I wasn't completely focused on Army life in those days. I ran the streets of Columbus to make up for all the time I had lost in training and while overseas. It was a GI town and had with it all the warts and seedy places that implies, especially in 1969. It was during one of those Columbus trips that I met Miss Gloria Smith while on a blind date. One of my buddies, Angelo Bianca, was dating a gal named Dolores and she suggested I come along on a double date, so the four of us went out for dinner. Gloria and I had made small talk and I felt like the date was going pretty well. Before I knew it, we were done and I was walking her to the car. Now was the time to make my move, or so I thought. I was mid-sentence telling her how much I enjoyed the date when she hopped in the car and rolled up the window and left me standing there. The next thing I knew the car was speeding off. It would be months before I saw her again. I came to feel that maybe the date didn't go so well after all.

My time in the Army was winding down and I had had just about enough of Woodruff. By now I had no intention of sticking around the Army. In my mind, I was going to make a point and I decided I was going to get out. Gloria and I had started dating and I expected that I would have other opportunities; I would just get a civilian job in Columbus and move on with my life. I felt that after three years in the Army, during which I gained confidence and overcame fears, that I could be successful at whatever I put my mind to. So as the days counted down to my freedom I had planned to just let the date come and I would just get out. I was just a few weeks into a new cycle of trainees when I relented and volunteered to stay in an extra month to get my final class through to graduation.

Then I left the Army. Just walked away. I let one man and his leadership style define me, and it drove me to a decision that I was not sure I was otherwise ready to make. I hung around Columbus looking for work during my final days in the Army, something they called terminal leave. I was still getting paid while I burned off some leave days. I was supposed to be looking for work, which I was, but I was getting frustrated with how poor the prospects for me were. I remember talking to a guy about a job and he offered me $1.25 to sweep floors. I told him he could shove his job, I could do better than that. But I couldn't. I was running out of time and running out of money. As the date of my final day in the Army loomed closer—and then passed—I knew I had to do something and I had to do it fast.

Anger is a funny thing. Some say anger is our body's signal to tell us we are out of control. It is an emotion that some let take control of them and use it to lash out at those we care about the most. I couldn't understand or comprehend those feelings, but at the moment Gloria had angered me and so there was nothing left for me to do in Columbus, Georgia.

I packed up my car and left. Capt. James G. Woodruff be damned, I was a proud fucking civilian again. Goodbye Army and to hell with you Gloria Smith, I'll show you. I pointed my Ford Fairlane towards Vancouver because I was finally going home. I showed them alright, one and all.

Understanding Tilley

*". . . soldiers want to be proud of their units, and the Army value
of loyalty militates against airing dirty laundry. Subordinates
might not report toxic leaders because nobody likes a whiner. We
expect professionals to perform to the best of their ability despite a
supervisor's leadership style. The Army inculcates an attitude that
one must respect the rank, even if one does not respect the person.
Military culture esteems technical competence, and technical
competence will lead some senior leaders to overlook flawed toxic
leaders."*

—Col. George E. Reed, U.S. Army
MILITARY REVIEW, July-August 2004

How does one overcome adversity and fear? As we
mature and gain more experience we become skilled at
managing life and work-related challenges, but what happens
when we are not yet equipped to deal with what may feel
like insurmountable challenges? Junior noncommissioned
officers and soldiers of today are often faced with dilemmas
like the one I faced at Fort Benning, and my situation shows
why leaders should clearly demonstrate in their actions their
concern for creating a balance between the mission and the
soldier. As compared to managers, leaders are expected to
inspire and influence. In my view, you do that in how you
go about creating relationships with your people. You build
their faith in your ability to lead, and in your actions, that
show that you really care for them. To me that is just another
way of saying that you work to gain their respect and trust.
Army leaders often have to be firm and unwavering in the
challenges of the profession— some might call it tough love.
But you can do that and still create an environment of give-
and-take, and you do that by fostering an open channel of

communication that builds a positive environment in which soldiers can grow and mature.

When faced at Fort Benning with a leader who lacked the respect of his people, I handled the situation by avoiding and dodging the issues. It was a different time and thankfully those types of relationships do not exist today. Or do they? Whenever two or more people are involved in a professional interaction there is the opportunity for tension to form between them, especially in a hierarchy like the military with many overlapping senior-subordinate roles. It doesn't take long for underlying factors like personality, lack of experience or judgement, or temperament to cause a misunderstanding or rift. If people do not address conflict head-on they may come to their own conclusions regarding the source of the tension, and they may default to real or perceived biases, like gender, sex, sexual orientation or religion. If there are differences in backgrounds, or if actions are taken without transparency or explanation, a conclusion might be drawn that such problems are due to something other than performance.

In hindsight, there were actions I could have taken back at Fort Benning, but for me at the time the most convenient method of coping was to just get as far away from my problems as quickly as I could. Keep out your feelers to judge whether people would rather serve with you or escape you. I was lucky to have the support of a competent and respected senior NCO in 1st Sgt. Johnson, although he was powerless to protect my attitudes about my commander and he had to suffer through this poor leader as well. Every day across the many formations there are events going on in the Army that are similar to my scenario. So, I ask, who are you going to be: the commander, the first sergeant, or Sgt. Tilley?

[5]

Anger Management

I took over 1st Battalion, 10th Cavalry from Jack when he became the 194th Armor Brigade CSM. He was an excellent Brigade CSM and I flourished under his leadership. We were athletically competitive and we both had fun with friendly competitions—we were even known to have push-up contests in our dress uniforms. When one would finish an event like a road race first (I think we're still 50/50 on who wins) the winner would gather a quick crowd to heckle the other. During that assignment, and others, I could tell from unit visits that his subordinate leaders and soldiers all admired and respected him.

—Cmd. Sgt. Maj. John Beck, U.S. Army, Retired
former Command Sergeant Major,
U.S. Army V Corps

January 17, 1970

Adjusting to life after combat is difficult for anyone, and ours was a different time in terms of understanding the stress it places on the mind. Maybe I was mad at the world or maybe I was just plain mad, but wrestling with anger is something that many returning soldiers are faced with. Yet then, and now, soldiers do not always feel comfortable talking about those feelings. There were names people used to describe soldiers who struggled with combat stress and they were often degrading or unsoldierly. One knew it was better to keep your demons locked inside and not talk much about it.

I pushed my combat experiences to the corners of my mind to help me live and cope with the memories that I was avoiding, and I was not one to dwell on the past. But here I was in January 1970, angry and irritated with the two most important elements in my life: the United States Army and Gloria Smith. I found myself detached and running away from my troubles instead of dealing with them head-on. At the moment, it seemed easier to leave the Army and Columbus, Georgia, than to deal with the people who had led me to that point. In looking back, it was clear that I lacked the skills to help myself cope with the anger inside.

Twenty-five hundred miles is a long way to drive. It gives a man time to think. I seem to recall that I couldn't wait to get back home, but the farther I drove that Fairlane the more I realized that there was not much waiting for me when I arrived. I had joined the Army to get away and to do something different and exciting, yet now I was driving headlong into the nothingness that I had tried to escape. It must have taken me four hours to reach Chattanooga, Tennessee, and it was there that I came to the conclusion that there was still one part of my life that I could regain control of: I knew I did not want to take this journey without Gloria.

So, I pulled the car over at the nearest payphone and called her to apologize, and then I dropped a bombshell. I asked, "If I come back will you marry me and come back to Vancouver with me?" Well maybe she had been thinking just as intensely as I had, or the thought of me leaving for good didn't sit well with her. But whatever it was she responded with an enthusiastic "yes," and that was all I needed to hear. I turned that car right around and made it back to her place in just about two hours as she packed to make the long trip alongside me.

We had not put much thought into the details of the trip; we were young and impulsive, and we figured things would simply work themselves out. It took days to get where we were going, but we didn't care because we were together again. We drove the nation's roads coast to coast for the first time and talked a lot about our futures, and what we planned to do. We were plagued with troubles along the way, and I had to deal with multiple flat tires. We didn't consider the weather as we left Columbus in January, but as we continued west the temperatures began to drop. We weren't prepared for cold and snow, and were especially concerned when the signs near the Rocky Mountains called for tire chains. I pushed ahead, taking the risk and hoping we wouldn't get caught. We just kept heading west.

Gloria had agreed to marry me, but we had not thought through the when and the how of our decision. We decided we wanted to be wed before we reached Vancouver, so we chose Nevada because of that state's lenient rules regarding marriages. It was January 16, 1970. The first major town west of Salt Lake City was Elko, so we stopped there and met with the justice of the peace and he helped us through the formalities of marriage. Before long we were on the way again as Mr. and Mrs. Jack and Gloria Tilley.

We settled in Vancouver, taking a room in a small two-story apartment in town. It wasn't much, but it was ours, and it was there that Gloria and I began our life together. Gloria went to work for the phone company while I bummed around town looking for work and collected an unemployment check. The Northwest in the winter of 1970 was a wild and wooly place, and in the neighborhood that we lived it wasn't unusual to smell the odor of marijuana wafting around the building, it was often coming from our downstairs neighbor. I spent my time drinking beer and shooting pool while the checks came rolling in, and I might be still be doing that today if the money hadn't all of a sudden dried up. I went to the unemployment office to find out what happened and that's when I learned that the benefits were only for a short time, a temporary crutch to help someone get on their feet. I had used mine up. I was unemployed with no money, and the reality of receiving only a portion of my final pay in my last unemployment check finally got me motivated to go out and look for a real job.

I first went to work for a paneling factory, working full-time and bringing in my share of money to our little family. I soon moved on to a job at a chemical plant, but I remained unsatisfied. I had started to think of how unfair it was that I had let Woodruff dictate how I was to live my life, especially since I had enjoyed what I was doing at Fort Benning as a soldier. I started hanging around the Vancouver recruiting station, befriending one of the recruiters and occasionally checking in on him and talking shop. I knew deep down I missed the Army, but I was too busy trying to be a civilian to do more than just talk. Yet just a few months later on a trip to Seattle I found myself drawn to Fort Lewis and the area where I had done my own training in what seemed a lifetime ago.

A drill sergeant saw me standing around watching, and came up to me wanting to know who I was, what was going on, and why was I standing in his area watching all this. I told him that I used to be a drill sergeant too and this was where I trained. So, we talked for a little while about the

Army. I was probably getting closer in my mind to knowing that I wanted to go back in the service, but I just wasn't ready to commit—at least not until the recruiter I had been talking with called me to say that if I wanted to reenter the military with the rank that I had, I needed to do it by the end of the week.

I was promoted to staff sergeant before I left the Army, and the thought of coming in as a private didn't sound very good to me, so I told him to draw up the paperwork and I would come back in the Army again. I took some time off from my job and went to Portland, Oregon, to take the required tests and receive the physical exams, and they swore me in to the Army. Just like that, I was going to be a soldier again, so I went back to my job and told my boss I was going to "retire." I left civilian life and never looked back.

February 12, 1974

I had been out of the service for almost two years, so I had to go to Fort Jackson, South Carolina, to be inducted back in to the Army. I was issued new uniforms and gear and I found myself reverting to the ways of the military pretty quickly; it was like I never left. When the sergeant in charge told us to form up, I just fell in line and did what the others did. That evening the 1st Sergeant called for me and asked me for my story, and I explained that I was prior service. He pointed to my empty collar and asked about my rank. Upon my telling him I was a staff sergeant, he told me to "double-time" over to supply to get some stripes.

The next time we lined up for formation one of the trainees saw me, this time with stripes on and standing at the back of the formation. He asked me "Hey, how did you get those stripes, why were you promoted?" I looked at him with a straight face and said, "Kid, you can do it too if you are on your best behavior." That soldier is probably still telling stories about this one private who got promoted to staff sergeant at the reception station "for being squared away."

After I processed back into the Army, Gloria and I were assigned to Fort Polk, Louisiana, where for the next two and a half years I again was responsible to train newly inducted soldiers as a drill sergeant with Company C, 5th Battalion, 1st Training Brigade. Portions of Fort Polk had dense, jungle-like vegetation, and this environment was a perfect place for the Army to prepare troops for the environment and climate of Southeast Asia. We had the recruits for their first eight weeks, during which we transitioned them from civilians to soldiers.

I loved my job and I enjoyed sharing my knowledge with these men, most of who would likely be shipping out to Vietnam. We taught them all the things they would need to know to be a soldier: how to march, how to use their weapons, military customs and courtesies, and above all, how to follow orders. I loved the physical conditioning we did and I would exercise along with them as we tried to toughen their minds and their bodies. Then we would ship most of them across post where they would attend Advanced Individual Training, during which they mostly lived in the base's wooded area learning advanced tactics and how to survive in the jungle. By most accounts more soldiers were shipped to Vietnam from Fort Polk than from any other American training base.

The number of men required for service for Vietnam was shrinking as U.S. troop commitments dropped. From a peak of 560,000 in 1968, by end of 1972 there were fewer than 25,000 American troops in country. It wasn't long before

Gloria and I fell into a routine not unlike what we knew at Fort Benning. We began to see some predictability and stability in our lives and we started thinking more of our future. Initially, I had entered the Army with no aspirations of making a career out of it; it was a goof and something for a bored teenager to do. After returning to civilian life, I knew that I was cut out for Army life, which is why I returned. In many cases the Army continued to challenge me, and I was usually surrounded by good people who were strong influences on me. I liked moving around, so the fact of not having to stay in one place for too long was appealing to me. I just now began to start thinking of the Army as not just job, but as a way of life.

I found myself surrounded with great noncommissioned officers and role models while at Fort Polk. I had begun to pick out leaders around me, both officers and noncommissioned officers, who I wanted to be like. Two that made a lasting impression on me were a couple of platoon sergeants, Sgts. 1st Class Langston and Mayes. These two were cool characters whose leadership styles and mannerisms were what I wanted to emulate and I am saddened that time and distance kept me from staying connected with them. One of the best pieces of advice Langston gave me was that the most important thing I could give a soldier was my time. I got to Fort Polk thinking I knew all that I needed to know because of my time "on the trail" at Fort Benning. But it was in working with the cadre of Charlie Company that I realized I would be best served by picking out a few good traits of people like Langston and Mayes, and then apply them to my own leadership style.

One of the differences between my two experiences as a drill sergeant was that I took a more professional approach to basic training the second time around. Though there are stories from veterans of the Vietnam era about the treatment of trainees (including outright abuse), I am not sure just how widespread it may have been. In 1967 the Army was leaning very heavily on draftees, and many going through the training centers were not there of their own free will. The drill sergeant program was in its infancy at the time and the Army was building fighters and growing at a rapid pace.

Because of that, we drill sergeants often had to get the job done as best as we saw fit. I know I didn't abuse trainees or see it happen, but I did have to be tough. Tough is not bad, but tough is tough. I may have hollered and shouted and used a few choice words that wouldn't ordinarily be used in public, but that was often because it seemed like the appropriate thing to do, a way to motivate the youth we were charged with. However, during my time at Fort Polk, the Army was getting smaller and the draft had ended, and conversion to an "All-Volunteer Army" had begun.

Though the draft ended in July 1973, Project VOLAR which started in 1971, was well underway in the early part of the 1970s. The majority of the trials were held at three U.S. bases, and much of what was tested was implemented at Fort Polk after the testing ended in 1972. Project VOLAR involved changing values, beliefs, and attitudes of soldiers of the World War II, Korean War, and the post-Vietnam generations. Many of the initiatives appealed to young draftees whom the Army needed to reenlist to maintain its strengths.

Many careerists felt the changes went too far, or that they cut to the core of maintaining good order and discipline. Along with intense scrutiny of the Army as a whole, the training centers, the drill sergeants, and the cadre who trained these new recruits were also under a microscope. Because of the increased focus on the nature of our training and how we developed new soldiers, I believed we had a higher caliber of noncommissioned officers serving as drill sergeants. We knew our leaders cared more and were watching us more closely than I ever recalled at Fort Benning; it was my opinion that the Army was heading in the right direction.

It wasn't too long after we settled in at Fort Polk that Gloria and I decided to start a family. Gloria got pregnant and went through the typical pregnancy, eventually delivering a baby boy whom we named Brian. Like any parents we were happy-go-lucky with the birth of our first child, going through the usual rituals and watching him grow. It was just fifteen months into Brian's young life in 1974 that the world stopped for us—our son began to unexplainably convulse. We took him to the emergency room at the Fort Polk hospital and realized the severity of his situation when we were told that they were not equipped to handle Brian's illness. He was medically evacuated to Fort Sam Houston in Texas and Gloria went along to care for him. It was there that we learned the diagnosis: pneumococcus meningitis. I thought to myself, this is it—his life is finished.

Meningitis is severe inflammation of the membranes covering the brain and spinal cord, and it can lead to serious long-term consequences if not treated quickly. The United States military had been plagued by meningococcal diseases at least since World War I, as the training environment is a ripe breeding ground for the easy spreading of the disease. It is passed from person to person and the transmission is facilitated by cramped living conditions, poorly ventilated barracks, rigorous physical training, exposure to the elements, and poor sleep cycles.

The military had to deal with meningitis at all times, but during peak mobilization cycles like wartime the number of cases grew. Though advances in medicine had made great strides, new strains caused incident rates in Vietnam-era trainees to exceed even World War II numbers. Meningitis outbreaks were so severe in 1964 that the Army closed Fort Ord, California, to recruit training for almost a year. By 1971 the Army had helped create a vaccine that was tested and approved for military trainees at places like Fort Polk, but it would not be until 1974 that a vaccine would be approved for the general public. Children and youth are most susceptible to the virus that causes the reaction; since immunizations were not yet widespread, like most children at the time Brian had not yet been immunized.

I was summoned to Fort Sam Houston to be with my family. We were a young couple living on meager wages and we did not have a lot of cash in reserve, emergencies like this could easily strain a budget. While I was completing a request to take "emergency leave" to be with my family, my first sergeant led a campaign among my coworkers to take up a collection; my comrades responded with cash donations. Before I left Johnson handed over a stack of bills and offered his words of support. It wasn't a loan—the guys wanted us to have the money to help defray costs, and the compassion those men had for my family and I overwhelmed me.

Once I arrived at Fort Sam Houston I realized that Brian's condition had gotten worse, he lost his vision and could not hear. When Gloria called for me I assumed it was so I could say my goodbyes. I was convinced that Brian was not going to make it. While the hospital staff was doing all that they could to treat him with antibiotics and anticonvulsants, he continued to fight. This went on for months, through many treatments and lengthy hospital visits. I was technically on emergency leave and we were living in temporary lodging nearby, but Gloria and I mostly stayed at the hospital watching over Brian. And praying.

It was during one of those treatments, and at the doctor's urging, that Gloria and I took some much-needed time for ourselves and had a weekend away from the hospital. She had been by Brian's side since the first seizures, and both of us had been helping with his care continuously. We used our little getaway time to recharge our batteries. After we returned we were sitting in the room with Brian while he was trying to play, and we became ecstatic when we saw him reach to pick something off the floor—a small piece of lint. We were overjoyed that he could see it because that meant he was regaining his eyesight.

The Army approved a "compassionate reassignment" for us to Fort Lewis, Washington. Such reassignments are considered when a medical facility is identified that is better equipped to care for cases like Brian's, so I returned to Fort Polk to gather our things and we transferred to Washington State. But even there Brian's condition worsened. He continued to suffer from the effects of the disease, which had progressed to encephalitis, a more advanced condition of meningitis. At the peak of his infection he was suffering through 20–30 convulsions a day and it again appeared to me that he was not going to make it. Watching my son fight through these attacks was too much to bear; what I saw would be pure anguish to any parent.

I remember going to the hospital chapel to be alone. I dropped to my knees and asked God to either let Brian live, or let him die. It wasn't fair that my young boy would have to endure a life of suffering. I felt it was hopeless and he shouldn't have to live under these conditions. Then without explanation his condition began to change. We began to gain hope. It hadn't been since my ammo can bible that I thought at much length about spirituality and God, but my faith had been restored and I knew in my heart that divine intervention helped pull Brian through. I asked the doctor what had changed and why he had got better, the doctor just shrugged it off. Brian's circumstances made me look at things so much differently in life and about what is really important.

I believe in the power of prayer and felt that Gloria and I were picked to survive this because we could. It was our strength and conviction that allowed us to endure the trials and tribulations of Brian's illness. And through his strength my son Brian changed my life. Even after much therapy and rehabilitation Brian still suffers the effects of the illness and remains hearing impaired, but thanks to treatment his seizures are now under control.

Understanding Tilley

Family is not an important thing. It's everything.
—Michael J. Fox

My son Brian changed my life. Because of him I look at things in life much differently and I understand what is important in life. I may have been a lot of things in the Army but I was not a reflection of a soldier who had balance between my career and my family. The Army's gung-ho attitude and "HOOAH" culture encourages, and rightly demands, an environment of "service above self." Even the NCO Creed demands that noncommissioned officers should know our Soldiers and "will always place their needs" above our own. But as people mature so do organizations, and today's doctrine specifically identifies a leader's responsibility for forming climates that allow subordinates an opportunity to balance personal needs with mission requirements.

Today the Army expects its leaders to balance between professional work and personal life, while still making time for developmental assignments and self-development opportunities throughout their careers. Though many well-intentioned leaders like myself spoke of those things, we often did not practice them in our own personal actions. It is time that we break out of the cycle of running good people into the ground, and in many cases, we need to quit making excuses for why we are not doing more than paying lip service to it. We all know that actions speak louder than words, so it is the leaders who need to act to solve this.

The military family is a valuable resource to a soldier, and that encompasses both immediate and extended family members. Spouses, children, parents, and siblings all are a part of the network that keeps soldiers grounded and encourages resiliency. Though we are all a Soldier for Life, we should aspire to live a life that allows our family to be beside us when we eventually finish our service obligations. We often hear the phrase that we enlist a soldier, but reenlist a family. In this day and age of shrinking force size, dwindling budgets, and a whole new round of "doing more with less," it is imperative that we continue to monitor requirements versus available assets, and be advocates to our leaders when demand outweighs supply. Sometimes it is easier to manage tangibles like supplies, beans, and bullets, but when it comes to human capacity there are limited resources.

Obviously, your goal should be to create fit and resilient soldiers who have stamina that can build or tap into reserves, so we leaders must monitor that in them and ourselves. Leaders must sometimes be the filter and serve as the honest broker, especially in how we manage our soldiers' time and activities. If we don't we run the risk of losing their trust and confidence, especially if it is for the wrong reasons. Soldiers want to know leaders "have their back," and take their needs into consideration either when making decisions or in receiving missions or orders from on high.

Many times, decisions are made outside of our control, and when this happens it is important to use your experience to employ the right amount of urgency, with tact, to explain the effects of those decisions to your leaders. This allows you to either garner support to make changes or mitigate risk, and lets them fully clarify their intent. In the end if they do not modify a decision then that is their signal that they accept the risk to proceed. It is then up to you to decide if you should press the issue, or accept it and move on. Regardless the outcome, be sure to close the information loop, when the mission dictates, by explaining the results to those most affected by the decisions.

[6]

Surveying the Rubble

During my very first meeting with Jack there was no question what he expected of not only me, but from all Soldiers. It did not matter if you were a private, an NCO, or an officer, his standards were the same. He first assured me that I was the right person for the job, but like any new position I would have challenges. He explained that the best way to handle these challenges was to always be a forward thinker and get ahead of the turmoil. I cannot count the number of times I was asked why a person of my position still got into foxholes and low-crawled with troops. My answer was always that it was because I learned from a great leader: Jack Tilley.

—Cmd. Sgt. Maj. Joe Gainey, U.S. Army Retired
1st Senior Enlisted Advisor to the Chairman of
The Joint Chiefs of Staff

How do you rebuild an Army that has been decimated by more than eight years of ground combat? Of the twenty-seven million men who were draft eligible between the peak ground combat years of 1964 and 1973, 40 percent were drafted into military service. The United States suffered more than 58,000 killed in action or as noncombat losses in Vietnam when the final draft call was issued on December 7, 1972.

There were programs instituted to help keep the draft numbers high, such as Defense Secretary Robert McNamara's Project 100,000. Created in 1966, it reduced the entrance standards to allow 100,000 men classified in the lower mental categories to enlist or be drafted per year. It was originally labeled as part of the president's "War on Poverty," as it was considered a method of giving training and education to the poor or uneducated.

We were faced with those who couldn't speak English or had little aptitude, and some even had physical impairments. By the conclusion of the American commitment in Vietnam in 1975 the Army had abolished the draft and reverted to an all-volunteer Army. It had disestablished the Woman's Army Corps and integrated women within the ranks. Only slightly aware of the big-picture moves going on around me, I remained busy being a soldier, a husband, and a father. I pressed on living the life of a sergeant in an Army that was confronting strife and change.

The Army faced turbulence in the 1970s. One area in which it had problems, just as the nation at large did, was in race relations. At the Department of Defense's direction in 1973 the services were required to establish a comprehensive education program in race relations for all members of the military. The nation had enacted the Civil Rights Act ten years earlier that ended segregation in public places and banned employment discrimination on the basis of race, color, religion, sex, or national origin.

That legislation included the United States military as well. Though Vietnam was the first racially integrated war fought by the United States since the American Revolution, many black leaders opposed it for many reasons. Some of them believed the draft and programs like McNamara's were destructive to the black community. Just because the ranks were integrated didn't necessarily mean that minorities were openly accepted by the predominantly white majority. Soldiers were soldiers, and human nature and societal forces affected relations between people of many different walks of life. Meanwhile, as a military force we just did what we always did; we changed and adapted.

Having returned to Washington State and Fort Lewis, I was assigned to the 9th Infantry Division "Old Reliables" as an 11E Tank Commander in February 1974. I was sent there to be near suitable medical facilities for Brian, and it would be my first operational unit since I left Vietnam. The division had been reactivated at Fort Lewis in May 1972 as part of the U.S. Vietnam drawdown; the 2nd Brigade of the 9th Division had recently returned after serving as the Army's part of the joint Mobile Riverine Force. The activation took place over a year and they brought an influx of over 8,000 new recruits into the division, and when fully manned it was classified as the "first all-volunteer division" in the United States Army. The 2nd Battalion, 77th Armor was a newly formed unit and had been designated a priority by the time I was assigned there. Though they had been filling the ranks with new soldiers, the unit had a shortage of experienced noncommissioned officers across the division, and the post staff was deeply involved in manning us to our authorized strength.

Over my many years of service I was continuously exposed to great leaders and people who inspired me, so I always tried my best to learn from those I met. Some lessons came from examples of strength or compassion; others came via tales of how *not* to lead. I consider myself a people person and I am always ready to talk with and learn from those I meet. I tried to treat people the same way I wanted to be treated.

The "Golden Rule" is a pretty good philosophy that I had come to embrace. I enjoyed being with soldiers and joked and had fun when and where I was able. We worked hard, but I also took time to have a good time and set the example for communicating, and I don't think that ever changed.

I am competitive by nature—whether it's boxing, football, pool, or push-ups, to me friendly competition is good for the soul and it is the bedrock of the things I find important. It was odd to me then that during an important stage of a tank commander's critical development, Tank Gunnery, I found myself at odds with a superior: my battalion commander. At the time I was an upbeat guy and I took my NCO duties seriously. I could usually get along well with people, so it was a blow to me when during tank gunnery my battalion commander would prove to be an example of a shallow leader. As far as I knew Lt. Col. Mark Reynolds[3] was an alright guy, but I was about to find myself in another defining moment of my personal development.

Fort Lewis–based units held large-scale exercises and gunneries at the Yakima Firing Center almost 200 miles to the east. Created in time for World War II and then shuttered afterwards, the Yakima Firing Center was reopened in 1951 and expanded to 261,000 acres. Its missions at the time varied from reserve training to the testing of field artillery equipment and munitions. This was to be the first year that Yakima hosted division-level exercises since World War II. It was during one of our gunneries that the tank I was on, an aging M60A1, had a malfunction and my crew and I could not complete our qualification run. At that point my battalion commander and I had not crossed paths very often; I was just another staff sergeant tank commander to whom he had not had to pay much attention.

[3] Not his real name

Tank gunnery is serious business and qualification is a make-or-break situation for leaders in tank units. Accurately knocking down targets is more than a source of bragging rights: Qualification and the processes leading up to the final runs are well orchestrated and monitored events. Qualifying crews was a top priority in 2/77 Armor, and over the years many a tank commander saw his career aspirations falter due to poor results at a tank range.

Main battle tanks are mechanical marvels: they are electrically and hydraulically operated, with controls fulfilling the specific purpose of rapidly delivering the tank's crew and firepower to a point on the battlefield so the commander can use them as the situation requires. Because of that, crews understand the need to keep these machines in top condition and maintenance is high on the list of the most important tasks the team must perform. However, even under the best circumstances equipment breaks at the most inopportune time, which is what happened to my tank. On that day we failed to qualify. Not qualifying is one of the worst-case scenarios for a tank commander, so equipment failures are closely monitored and identified.

To the Army's credit there is a process to review the circumstances when such failures happen. This process exists because a number of variables come in to play during training that may be artificial to battlefield conditions, or because of factors beyond the operator's control such as target or weapon system malfunctions. Because I had such a malfunction, I requested to appeal my qualifying run. In my case the tank had a serious and unexpected mechanical problem, and as such the scorers recognized it was beyond the control of my crew and me. After the range operators reviewed our specific circumstances, they allocated a redo, or what is known as an "alibi" run. The problem was corrected and my crew had the opportunity to requalify, and we went on to shoot high tank.

Achieving the top tank score is a special accomplishment for a crew, especially when it's a tank commanded by a hotshot staff sergeant, which I considered myself. Though the honor is usually short-lived, the top firing crews are usually held in high regard and often can be heard around the chow hall or in the motor pool talking shit and bragging on their prowess when it comes to fire and maneuver. It was to my surprise, and against my protests, that after our top score I was immediately assigned to the crappiest of all range details—a task usually left for the less inclined. My reward for being high tank was pulling "ammo guard." Instead of basking in the glory alongside my buddies, I was stuck alone with my detail, unsure of what the hell was going on and why had I been knocked down a few pegs for fatigue duty. If this was some sort of lesson I was to be taught I had no clue what it was all about.

I later found out that the battalion commander had directed I pull ammo guard, which seemed like a chicken shit maneuver to pull. Instead of congratulating us it seemed Reynolds resented my appealing our run. I will never know since he never approached me nor explained why he changed what had been the norm for high gunnery scores. It's not that I felt I deserved awards or accolades, but it seemed to me that the trait of a positive leader would be to recognize and call out my crew with a pat on the back or a simple "good job."

It could have gone a long way. As part of my evolving views on the role and importance of leader skill I had come to believe in the importance of talking with soldiers and encouraging them to get the best performance out of them. And, if they faltered, not belittle them, but provide advice and counsel on ways to do better the next time, and show them ways to improve. This was not the case for me then, and I fumed and added the experience to my kit bag as another lesson on how *not* to lead soldiers.

As in my past, events like this caused me to question my calling and wonder if the Army was right for me; in fact, the situation was not much different from my disagreement with my company commander at Fort Benning. I felt to my core that healthy competition was a way to motivate soldiers and leaders to accomplish what we asked them to do, but in this case my commander did not support me and my style. Leadership is fairly well defined, but the way each individual delivers his or her own brand is uniquely personal.

I believed my commander chose to "develop" me in a way that seemed unfair and created distrust between us. I had matured and developed since my Fort Benning days, but I again found myself in the middle of a situation that had not gone my way. How I felt about Reynolds's puzzling reactions was in many ways similar to how I felt about the problems that had happened to Brian and my family: I concluded that "It's not fair that these things keep happening to me." I asked myself "Why did this happen? I'm a good guy and I do things that are right." I knew I had to come to grips with life's trials and tribulations and decide whether I even wanted to stay in the Army.

I have come to realize that it is through the strength of my family that I could take on the challenges that life has given me. God selected me to do those tasks. Spirituality is not something that I wore on my sleeve. However, my faith in a higher power is what has helped me stay grounded and maintain my confidence in myself during my most challenging times. In explaining Brian's condition, an acquaintance once

told me that "special children have special families." I let
that sink in, and doing so allowed me to draw comfort in
her words. It was through my own assurances that I knew a
higher power, God. I had belief that our family could handle
the challenges and I began to understand my own strength.
Actually, it's been through Gloria's strength that we have
overcome each challenge. I was just lucky enough to be able
to hold on and draw my strength from her.

As Brian's condition stabilized, Gloria and I were better
equipped to help care for him and we were given the green
light for an overseas assignment. There was no Exceptional
Family Member Program, it would be five or six years later
that the Army would create specialized programs for families
that had unique, but manageable special needs members.
The military lifestyle can follow a rocky path, but it is an
experience unlike other professions. With overseas service,
long separations, and fears of deployments and wars, a soldier's
spouse, children, and extended family are in a constant cycle
of ups and downs.

Previous generations may have known lulls during the
interwar periods but it is clear that today's families are faced
with challenges similar to those we faced. It is the soldier's
spouse that often serves as the anchor that holds the family
together. For Gloria it was often more difficult for her to
hold a job or socialize because of her desire to be there for
Brian, and later for our younger son, Kevin. I was grateful for
the fact that she allowed me to be a soldier and to do some
of the important things in my life. As we finished our Fort
Lewis assignment, I felt it important that we share some time

together as a family so we took a trip to Myrtle Beach, South Carolina, for a family getaway.

I was excited to go back overseas; at least this time I would be going with family, and to a more hospitable place. We were heading to Aschaffenburg, Germany where I was to be reassigned to another a tank battalion. I was looking forward to the opportunity, but a bit reluctant. Coming out of Fort Lewis I laid back a bit to improve the chances that I could go over as a senior staff sergeant and be assigned as a tank commander to refine my skills as a noncommissioned officer. At that time, it seemed only the "cream of the crop" went to Germany because there was a lot of competition for what was a favorable posting for tankers—the European theater was the place to be. I was glad to have been given the opportunity to go, but still fresh on my mind were the experiences like those with my battalion commander.

Still not overly concerned about making rank, I knew that if soldiers did their job well that they were sure to be selected for promotion. I was a senior staff sergeant by now but had never filled out a packet for an Army centralized promotion board. At that time we had the choice to compete for promotion or not; your intentions were signaled by your taking action to put together your personnel records and acknowledging you wanted to be considered for promotion. I had always seen myself as getting the right opportunities but I never was promoted ahead of my peers. I believed that as a staff sergeant in a platoon sergeant position my superiors would be more forgiving of mistakes than if I was a sergeant first class. This line of thinking was probably more of a lack of confidence in my own abilities and I did not feel I was yet qualified to be a platoon sergeant. The last thing I wanted to do was to go to a new assignment only to embarrass myself and get relieved. The pressure was on.

Understanding Tilley

When implemented consistently by conscientious officers and NCOs, the (Project Volunteer Army) initiatives often resulted in soldiers' being treated like mature adults and not like children, with a concomitant increase in pride, morale, and reenlistment rates.
—Richard W. Stewart,
American Military History, Volume II

I don't believe over the span of my career that I changed much in the way I deal with people. It may have sucked getting older, but I was the same leader as a sergeant as when I was a sergeant major. When people look back on me I hope they are able to say that I worked hard and did my job well. I often used humor and levity to display the joy I felt in soldiering; it was true that I liked to have fun but I continued to work at setting the highest example. I believe that I did the best that I could, and I don't believe that I changed much throughout my career. I believe in life, I believe in the strength of prayer, and I believe that our military does things right each and every day. I wish our country could see that more often.

Coming up through the ranks I made it a point to visit soldiers where they lived. I walked the barracks or ate with them on weekends and holidays. To me acts like that were important. I would come in primarily to see how my soldiers were getting along, and oftentimes this consisted of nothing more than watching cartoons on a Sunday morning. People knew I was there and they were accustomed to seeing me around, and so they would talk to me because I would take that extra two to three hours to interact. When you sit down on the edge of a bed or in a chair in a soldier's room, or play foosball or a game of pool with somebody, you're in their house. And they understand whether you're real or you're Memorex. Soldiers understand that you are there not because you have to be there, but because you really, sincerely care about them. They figure it out real quick through your actions.

Don't just talk about taking care of soldiers, "Take care of Soldiers!" Learn about them and their families and what makes each of them tick. The closer you are to them in the supervisory chain, the more you need to know—and remember, we work two levels down. Learn about what they're doing with their free time. If you are a good sergeant first class, you stay focused on your platoon. Do the kinds of jobs that support your chain of command. Too often people get so wrapped up in getting their next stripe or getting the next position that they lose focus about what they're really supposed to be doing, which is taking care of that section or squad or platoon or company. That is what you are responsible for, so focus there first. Experience turns soldiers into leaders, and a way to be a good leader is to lead with integrity. Learn from those around you because to be a good leader you must also be a good follower. From what I've seen, development and expertise comes with time, so use your time wisely. If you consistently do it right, the rest will come.

[7]

Fresh Starts and Farewells

RELENTLESS describes Jack Tilley. Jack was relentless when pursuing what he believed would help his soldiers. He would always interpret or argue for interpreting and even changing regulations and rules to favor the troopers of his battalion, his Army, or of all the Military Services of the United States.
> —Cmd. Sgt. Maj. David L. Lady, U.S. Army Retired
> former Command Sergeant Major,
> U.S. Army, Europe

March 16, 1976

We were assigned to West Germany at a time when the Berlin Wall existed, and when there were two U.S. corps worth of military might protecting the Fulda Gap, the perceived avenue of entry for Warsaw Pact armor attacks should world war break out in Europe again. It was a unique experience for GIs of many generations. I served at Ray Barracks in Friedberg with the "Iron Dukes" of the 3rd Battalion, 32nd Armor Regiment of the 3rd Armored Division. Ray Barracks was the same post that Elvis Presley served during the late 1950s; he served with our sister 1/32nd Armor Battalion and met his future wife Priscilla in Bad Nauheim, only a few towns away.

It was with the 3rd Armored Division that I had the chance to grow and flourish, and to really understand the roles of the noncommissioned officer. I was initially sent to join the 3rd Infantry Division at Ready Barracks as a tank commander with 4th Battalion, 64th Armor Regiment, but the medical facilities were not adequate to care for Brian so I was reassigned to 3/32nd Armor as a tank commander. I moved to Headquarters Company for a short time to be a section leader and I quickly got into a groove. Soon after I arrived to Germany and observed the caliber of the NCOs around me I knew I measured up. I was as good as they were, and this convinced me to make sure my personnel records were ready to go for the next board.

Just three years after the end of major hostilities in Vietnam and barely a year since the fall of Saigon, the Army was a service unsure of itself or its future. In early 1977 a joint message by the Secretary and Chief of Staff of the Army stated the primary mission of the U.S. Army was to prepare for battle in Central Europe against the forces of the Warsaw Pact, and as such our activities during my assignment were geared toward that preparation. There were alerts and gunneries, field exercises and training—an experience shared by many "Cold War" warriors who soldiered overseas in the post-World War II era.

Initially my platoon sergeant was Sgt. 1st Class Richard Wilson. He had been a recruiter and he had been away from being in tank platoons, but I really admired his leadership style. He taught me a lot about leading a platoon. I was made a tank commander and Wilson matched me up with a soldier named Arlie Pyles. Our personalities clicked right away and we eventually became one of the best tank crews in that unit. Arlie and I became great friends and he was also someone I came to admire. We spent a lot of time in the field perfecting our skills, and it was always a big deal to us to have the best qualifying runs. Because of the chemistry between Arlie and I we once scored a perfect "run" during tank gunnery. We were that good together and we were leading our section. Each tank platoon had two sections and the other section was weak, so Wilson split Arlie and me up so he could have parts of his best crew in both sections. In the end we both went on to have great runs and the platoon got through. As a section Arlie and I would have fired and shot everything down, but the other section would have bolo'd.[4] At first, we were pissed off about the split, but in hindsight I would have done the same thing if I was in Wilson's shoes because it was the right thing to do for the unit. He was more concerned about the bigger picture and the unit's overall success, not our egos. I chalked that up as another important lesson from a wise NCO.

I considered myself able to get along with everyone and race was of little significance to me; I just liked connecting with all people. But in December 1975 Arlie and I were out at the NCO Club celebrating our birthdays. We were all fired up, drinking shots and then throwing our glasses on the ground just to hear them break. There was an African American soldier nearby and I noticed he was harassing a waitress and trying to get her to go out with him. I saw she was trying to fend him off so I hollered out to him to leave her alone, which he did, but he wasn't happy about me interfering. I was sitting there eating when he got up and walked to the bathroom, all while staring me down. I took my eye off of him and when he returned he jumped me. He leaped over a table throwing punches, but only ended up scratching me.

We threw down and started yelling at each other and the guy challenged me to go outside, which I stupidly did.

---

[4] Bolo is a slang term used when someone fails to qualify with a weapon or weapon system.

I didn't notice that he had grabbed a knife. As soon as I got outside he lunged at me. First he stabbed me in the side, resulting in a surface wound that took three stitches. Then he stabbed at my face, scraping the knife across it. Holy hell did that one hurt—then the shit hit the fan. The bar had called the fight in to the military police who showed up and broke us up and we were both hauled in to the station. I was sent to the hospital for treatment and ended up having to file a report on the incident. The military police arrested the guy and booked him.

Soldiers of my unit, both white and black, wanted blood, they felt the attack was racially motivated and told me I should press charges on the guy for attempted murder. More than a few of my friends were angry on my behalf. But I didn't see it that way, I told them it was a just a barroom brawl between soldiers, something that happens all the time. One or two of them tried to talk me out of it, trying to convince me it had to do more with race and color, but I knew better than that. I told my chain of command that I did not want to press charges and we went our separate ways. Sometimes soldiers are soldiers and do stupid things, especially when alcohol or romance are involved.

I was ultimately selected for promotion. After my selection to sergeant first class I was sent to Bravo Company where I served out my assignment as a platoon sergeant and was eventually promoted to sergeant first class. I was now an Army platoon sergeant in Europe, and all was right in my world. I had begun to come into my own leadership style, one that I created by watching the professionals around me. As I spread my own wings I now understood that most people are generally good deep down and if they make a common mistake in peacetime or in training that it is just that, a mistake.

I enjoyed being a soldier and one of my greatest pleasures was being among like-minded people. I continued to feed my competitive side and I even got back into boxing again while in Germany, working with a fighter who eventually went on to be an all-Army boxer. Competition and physical fitness, coupled with my own brand of plain talk, were the strengths I held dear, and they helped me be a better soldier. Too many times I had been around leaders who wouldn't look a soldier in the eye or would talk down to them; it was as if they were lesser people to that individual. To me it wasn't just about talking to soldiers, it was about talking with them.

I never thought that I had changed my leadership style over my career. I was the same person as a hard-stripe sergeant as I was when I was the Sergeant Major of the Army. Initially I might have thought yelling and hollering was a way to get young soldiers to respond, but by now I was beginning to learn to take time to talk with and explain myself to my soldiers. I saw that they responded much better. In hindsight I thought by the time I became a platoon sergeant I was a pretty good section sergeant, and later when I became a first sergeant I figured I knew the job of a platoon sergeant cold. That happens sometimes as you come through the ranks— you get to the next level and think "Crap, I wish I would have done *that* differently." With maturity and age, I learned that I was much better prepared to mentor and develop people as I progressed to higher levels. It was a lesson that I was just starting to learn, and one that would ring true throughout my career.

January 29, 1979

Upon my return to the United States, the Army selected me to serve as an instructor at the then "Home of Armor,"

Fort Knox, Kentucky. The installation is best known as the nation's gold bullion depository, which has been in operation since 1937. The base has been a permanent Army garrison since 1932. It became the center for mechanized tactics and doctrine and in 1957 became the U.S. Army Armor Center and served as the home of Cavalry and Armor until 2005. During the Vietnam buildup, it was one of the eight major Army Training Centers providing basic combat training and advanced individual training.

I was assigned to the 1st AIT/OSUT Brigade's Committee Group where at Fort Knox much of the technical training was conducted using the same type of instruction as I had experienced at Forts Benning and Polk; I would experience the other perspective of training the newly inducted by joining the special teams of military instructors teaching specific subjects. Basic trainees were rotated through these instructional committees, with the company drill sergeants filling the role of assistant instructors. Not all instruction was given by committees and many subjects such as drill and ceremonies were taught by company cadre without committee participation.

I was initially assigned to teach the basic fundamentals on the M1911 .45-caliber pistol, the tanker's primary sidearm. I was partnered with a more experienced soldier and I was assigned to teach pistol marksmanship at the Holder Range Complex. I did that for a few months before it was my turn to rotate to be a standard "platform" instructor. As committee members we did not teach only one subject, so I eventually qualified on many of the weapon systems such as the .50-caliber machine gun, and I also taught land navigation. One of the benefits I felt the soldier received in "learning by committee" was that it provided for standardized instruction that all soldiers had to master before they could move on to the next task.

I was enjoying what I was doing as a senior instructor, but then I got word that I was going to have a small part in what at the time was a revolutionary advance in military hardware: I was going to help create the program of instruction for the first group of recruits to train on the soon-to-be-fielded XM1 main battle tank. The Army had taken delivery of its first 110 XM1 tanks in February 1980 and final testing was going on at Fort Hood, Texas and Fort Knox before they would begin delivering the tanks to field units. Radical in design, the M1, as it would become known, was nicknamed the "Abrams" after legendary Armor officer and former Army Chief of Staff Creighton W. Abrams Jr. It was one of the three major combat systems fielded in the early 1980s—the other two were the Apache helicopter and the M2 Bradley Fighting Vehicle—to provide the U.S. Army increased and modernized fighting power.

The first units were not scheduled to begin receiving M1s until 1982. Our assignment was to come up with the lesson material for the newly created armored crewman specialty code "19K," and the one-station unit training (OSUT) program. OSUT was a new concept created for cost savings. The Army's traditional training of recruits had been conducted at two installations, with basic training at one station and advanced individual training at another. OSUT combined all the training at one site and in the same unit, thus reducing the time needed to train and saving millions of dollars per year. The Army had been studying the concept since the mid-1970s, but it was not until 1979 that it was done on a larger scale. Now I was a part of the team of officers and noncommissioned officers helping to apply this program to a relatively new piece of equipment.

I worked for almost a year planning and preparing before we finally received our first group of students. Though the first phases of OSUT mostly mirrored the basic training cycles that were happening elsewhere in the brigade, it was after an OSUT company finished the traditional combat training that the time that trainees spent with drill sergeants decreased, and the time they spent with the tank commanders and cadre increased. I was there as part of that first cycle when we conducted the first 19K OSUT tank gunnery in the Army.

My first sergeant of Company C went on leave. So the company commander called me to the orderly room to stand in for him. When the battalion got wind of the temporary move the battalion commander told my CO that if he can afford to take me out of training to be an acting first sergeant then he must not need me that bad, so the battalion commander pulled me to the staff to be his battalion operations sergeant. The position of operations sergeant was a master sergeant position, so I was pretty excited for the opportunity.

It was my first time on a staff and I came to relish my role. I was quickly immersed in many of the responsibilities, though there was little preparation for the work I was to undertake. It was still four years before the creation of the Army Operations and Intelligence Course, the precursor to today's Battle Staff NCO Course. I toiled away learning the finer points of staff operations and helping manage the planning and preparation that goes into unit operations. I was exposed to new aspects of the military decision-making process that I had not previously considered. And I loved the challenge.

October 26, 1982

After more than a year and with much griping and bitching on my part, a first sergeant position finally came open in Bravo Company. Bravo was the same company that I worked in while helping create the 19K OSUT program, and now I was returning to be its top noncom. Soon after arriving I met my company commander—the first of two I would serve with in Bravo Company—and told him that I might need his help because I had never been a first sergeant before. I was a sergeant first class still wearing those stripes, but I was now about to serve as the senior NCO of a company with what I thought was only a moderate amount of experience. My commander looked at me and laughed and said he had never been a captain before, so how about we pull together and get through the challenge as a team?

He was a great commander who was eager to succeed, and he and I got along well together—but he was also a hothead who was easy to get worked up. I remember one of his many outbursts in which he took out his rage on his phone, slamming it down on his desk until he broke it. He sat and stewed for a few minutes until he realized that he still needed to make his call, and he sheepishly came in to my office to try to use my phone. I picked it up and put it in my desk drawer and slammed it shut. I told him he had broken his phone and he damn sure wasn't going to break mine.

An OSUT company is unique in that we had all the trainees going through training, as well as the drill instructors who were on hand to lead them through the "soldierization" process. We also had cadre, those tank commanders who taught the basic fundamentals of tank operations to trainees, but distinctly different from the Committees. The selection process for a drill instructor was much more selective than for the tank commander cadre. I felt the drill sergeants were the cream of the crop of noncommissioned officers; the tank commanders, not so much.

The tank commanders were mostly solid soldiers and decent people, but the drill sergeants we had assigned were of a higher caliber. And because of the training methods of OSUT—where the drill sergeants did much of the hands-on individual training to be a soldier and care for the trainees morning, noon and night, seven days a week—the tank commanders typically had regular 9-to-5, five-day-a-week training cycles. Though the work hours would often cause friction, drill sergeants received incentive pay to somewhat compensate for that extra work, which the tank commanders did not let them forget.

Soon after taking over my duties I saw there was a crack in the relationship between the cadres. I knew we needed to be a cohesive team to be successful. I tried to pull the groups together and to talk and meet with the individuals from each group. A training company like Bravo was almost 100 percent mid- to senior-grade noncommissioned officers, other than a few in the headquarters such as supply specialists or administration "shadow" clerks. We were fairly lean and did not have a large staff or any extra positions, so mostly we had drill sergeants and tank commanders, staff sergeants and sergeants first class.

I realized a root of the problem was that most drill sergeants had not been cadre tank commanders, and most tank commanders had not been drill sergeants, so I decided to create a company-wide exchange program. For a cycle I would take a few drill sergeants and tank commanders and switch them out. A tank commander would perform the drill instructor's duties, and the drill sergeants would work with the trainees on the tanks, which was important for many of them because they had yet to experience the newly fielded tank. This allowed both groups to empathize with the challenges of the other, and get a better sense of the other's responsibilities. In the end it worked: the camaraderie of B Company soared.

It was during this tour that I had my first opportunity to attend an NCO school, the First Sergeant Course at the Army's Sergeants Major Academy in Fort Bliss, Texas. Professional military education, or the lack thereof, was an issue for the enlisted force of my era, and the creation and maturity of the noncommissioned officer education system is in my mind one of the most important things to have happened to our Army in its recent history. Though there was a scattering of unit-based schools or academies, it was not until 1957 that the U.S. Army even attempted to standardize leadership training for noncommissioned officers.

Even then that was hit or miss, and sometimes soldiers were forced to attend the same schools at different locations. And worse, often the wrong people (those who were "expendable") attended when mandatory quotas were created, as those who could surely benefit were deemed too important to their units to send. There was not a requirement—no one really pushed schooling, and it was not mandatory or a part of the career path. It would not be until 1986 that the Army tied education to promotions, thus making it mandatory. As a product of the system that I was faced with, I was glad to have been given the opportunity. At the time the NCO Education System had five levels: primary, basic, and advanced levels; the first sergeants course; and the sergeants major course. The 1986 changes removed the first sergeants course from the progression path.

After initial training the only military courses I had attended were Airborne School, Drill Sergeant School, and the Master Gunners Course. All of those courses were oriented as technical or "performance-oriented" training. The first sergeants course of the time was less training and more like formal education; it was more of a thinking and sharing of experiences course, not unlike what you might experience on a college campus. The best aspect for me was the interaction with the others attending the course, as the people I came in contact with were all great leaders; some I continued to stay in contact with throughout my career. One of the lessons I took from the program throughout the remainder of my time in the Army was that I felt I could always determine which first sergeants had or had not attended the course by their level of stress or anxiety. I felt that the resident first sergeant course gave the company, battery, and troop's most senior sergeants added confidence in themselves.

I spent more than seven years at Fort Knox during an influential developmental period for me, roughly the midway point in my career. I had the opportunity to hone my skills as a tank commander and be a part of new and emerging concepts and principles as the Army was rebuilding itself through investments in its equipment and personnel. I learned long-lasting lessons from a great crop of noncommissioned officers. One of those tremendously valuable people was the sergeant major of first battalion that I initially served with, Cmd. Sgt. Maj. John Kearns.

Kearns taught me a lot about leading soldiers and how to be responsible for your own actions. He wanted his first sergeants to know how to carry themselves and to be good role models and speakers. Once he tasked me with being a guest speaker at an upcoming OSUT graduation and I recall not being too keen on the idea. I believed that I was too busy to mess with a speaking role so I instead coaxed a fellow first sergeant to fill in for me. I went back to Kearns and explained, "Hey, sergeant major, I got Alpha Company first sergeant to fill in for me. Don't worry, he's got it covered." He about blew a gasket. He told me, "I didn't tell him to do it, I told you. Now do it and you don't get a choice, now get outta here." I got the message loud and clear and did what he asked. In the end a number of people came up to me and told me they enjoyed my speech and I continued to speak at graduations.

I was eventually selected to serve as the Basic Noncommissioned Officer Course (BNCOC) Chief Instructor at the Fort Knox NCO Academy and would finally get selected for promotion to master sergeant. I had already served as an operations sergeant and a first sergeant, both E-8 slots, and now I was finally getting the pay to go along with it. While there I had the chance to work with a major influencer on my career, Cmd. Sgt. Maj. John Stephens. I served as his tank commander during a training simulation once when he was the post command sergeant major, and for some reason he took the time to help shape and mentor me.

As the Armor Center and School CSM he had his thumbprints on many activities affecting not just Fort Knox but the entire enlisted career fields of armor and cavalry. He and his bosses were on the cutting edge of change. He served as the top NCO at Fort Knox for six and a half years and he provided me great advice and counsel, as well as the occasional swift kick in the butt when I needed it most.

As the BNCOC Chief I was responsible for providing oversight and management to the various basic NCO courses that we had underway for enlisted soldiers in the armor, cavalry, and infantry career fields. In this mostly administrative position I was a pencil pusher who oversaw the training and development side of the course management. It was during this time that Stephens tasked the academy and I to rewrite the entire M1 tank commander 19K BNCOC program of instruction, no small feat because of the complexity of the M1 tank. As sad as I was as this assignment came to a close, it was bittersweet: I had been selected to attend the U.S. Army Sergeants Major Academy, the capstone leadership school for Army sergeants.

Understanding Tilley

Leadership is intangible, and therefore no weapon ever designed can replace it.

—General of the Army Omar N. Bradley

It was an inspiring senior enlisted leader who focused me on doing the things that were important. He taught me that you can be successful at any job that you do while never leaving your office, but that's not what it's all about. Sometimes leaders talk about "taking care of soldiers" —well, part of taking care of soldiers is knowing them, counseling them, making sure that they're professionally developed for the next step or the next level in the line. My advice to aspiring company-level noncommissioned officers is that one of the most important things you can do is establish the atmosphere within your unit through leading by example.

Establish the climate by talking with your subordinate leaders; you cannot foster relationships by building a wall between you. This means that you do not create an attitude that shows "I'm the first sergeant, you're just a platoon sergeant." No one is less a person than I am; we're all at the same level. Sometimes people have a tendency of talking down to junior soldiers, so be careful not to let that happen. Words are important and you never really know when what you say is taken to heart, especially if it is harsh or demoralizing. Canadian writer Robin S. Sharma reminds us that "Words can inspire. And words can destroy. Choose yours well." Make sure your words convey the message you intend, but do so by choosing your words carefully.

Don't ever get stuck behind your desk, get out and be among your people. It was Gen. George Patton who said

"No good decision was ever made in a swivel chair," and I completely agree. Soldiers like when you are out among them, they prefer leaders who are out and about dealing with their issues and concerns. Work hard at being a part of the team versus trying to segregate yourself because of your rank or position. Unsuccessful company leaders allow themselves to want to do those things in the orderly room, versus being out with the soldiers. Do the things that soldiers do: participate in physical fitness training with them and their unit, eat in the dining facility, and exercise in the gym. Those are the actions that soldiers want to see you at, not sitting behind your desk all day. You should do those things at all hours of day, in the rain and the heat and the muck, day or night. When the lone outpost, the remote site, or the small formation is unexpectedly visited by its leaders when the circumstances are at their least favorable, it truly shows the stuff you are made of.

Barney and me heading to Vietnam

SSG Ahsbahs and me, and two long forgotten comrades
(photo courtesy Dan Thompson)

Me on the right digging in tank A25
(photo courtesy Dan Thompson)

Me on the left checking the "ma deuce"
(photo courtesy Dan Thompson)

Drill Sergeant Tilley

A Drill Sergeant work-out

While a student at the Sergeants Major Academy

An NCO led ceremony with the 1st Armored Division

Casing the 1st Armored Division colors enroute to Bosnia

Outside the Headquarters in Tuzla, Bosnia-Herzegovina

Gen. Eric Shinseki swearing me in as the 12th Sergeant
Major of the Army, with Gloria and Brian looking on

Doing one-armed push-ups

Posing with former SMAs Richard Kidd, George Dunaway,
Bill Bainbridge and Bob Hall

The senior enlisted advisors of each of the services and
me with the Honorable William Cohen and his wife
Janet Langhart

My family joining me before my retirement ceremony

Ted Hacker and me at the Ernest N. Morial Convention
Center in New Orleans, LA

[8]

Ultima

My impression of Jack Tilley has not changed since I first met him, and that was that he had "The Art of Leadership" written all over him. What some may recognize as dynamic, to him was business as usual. He was always available, not for himself, but for the Soldiers of the United States Army. His communication skills are second to none and I have had commanders come to me and talk about him like he was a recent miracle to arrive in their organization. He was about soldiers and he was comfortable being challenged and him challenging others. It was not just push-ups, it was talking about challenges and failures that exist in every command the Army has. Jack would have been successful whatever path he decided to take.
—Cmd. Sgt. Maj. John M. Stephens, U.S. Army Retired
former Command Sergeant Major,
U.S. Army Armor Center

August 4, 1986

At the time I attended the Sergeants Major Course it was the pinnacle of enlisted education. Attending the course was an exciting and anxious time in any soldier's career. The intense six-month program immersed senior NCOs from all services in all things necessary to assume duties as an operations sergeant major in a field unit or a joint assignment. Graduation from the course was often a discriminator for promotion to sergeant major. It was also a career ender for a few unprepared leaders—the last thing anyone wanted to do was to flunk out of the Sergeants Major Course.

Created in 1972, the U.S. Army Sergeants Major Academy was initially designed as an academic institution conducting education programs for senior noncommissioned officers; that specific program is now titled the Sergeants Major Course (SMC). This unique academy is located on a former U.S. Air Force base in El Paso, Texas, Biggs Army Airfield. It is now known as East Fort Bliss, and it has undergone a number of changes and enhancements since its creation.

Unlike other noncommissioned officer courses in which a soldier would leave his or her home base and attend in a "temporary duty" status, students at the SMC were detached from their unit and completed a permanent change of station to the academy. Upon completion, graduates would be put in a pool with their fellow graduates and be eligible for worldwide assignment. Oftentimes soldiers would pack up all their worldly possessions and move themselves and their families to Fort Bliss; however, because of Brian's health we felt that he could get better care at Fort Knox, so I moved Gloria and the kids to Elizabethtown, Kentucky, just right down the highway from Fort Knox, and away I went to join the 28th class.

El Paso and the Sergeants Major Academy were not new to me, as I had spent time there during the First Sergeants Course. Much of the teaching methods were the same between the two courses: There was small group instruction where a facilitator would lead discussion on a series of subjects, and students would inject personal experiences and observations into the dialogue. It was through these sessions that students would learn and grow. There was a lot of reading and writing and other scholarly activities such as preparing research papers and doing country studies, all of which offered us a university-like experience in many subjects outside the typical technical or tactical training of Army NCO Academies.

Because of the course intensity and since most of the students were approaching or had exceeded the twenty-year service mark and were far from their school days, students were required to take courses to build better study habits. One of the few problems I saw there was that many of my classmates could best be classified as "Type A" personalities, and I considered myself in that same group. Personalities like ours just want to get it done and get back to our units or our families. Though it was a six-month opportunity to slow down and take a little break or regroup and work on developing ourselves, it seemed many of us would have been just as happy to cut the course down to two weeks, get the required information, and move out. The way I looked at it is that we had worked hard throughout our military careers, and now was a chance to take a little bit of time to get rejuvenated, and then go back out to the force a better leader.

Adding to the stress were the exams. We would study for weeks and months and then at the end of a block we would be given a comprehensive exam. Oftentimes we would test in the morning and the exams would go out to be graded. Sometimes we wouldn't know whether we passed or failed until late in the evening. For one exam I didn't even find out; I ended up going to bed not sure how I did. I went in the next morning and told my small-group instructor there had to be a better system, that the anticipation was driving me bonkers. So he devised a system where at the conclusion of our test we would write down the letter of each answer (they were multiple-choice questions) and leave the key on our desk, and when the exam was over the class would review each question and we could usually see how we did.

Another benefit was the opportunity to work with many quality noncommissioned officers, including those from various branches and specialties. Up until now I primarily was assigned to armor and training units and I had been scarcely exposed to the service and support career fields. I enjoyed talking with and interacting with soldiers of so many different occupational specialties. These conversations were the richest reward of attending the course, and I formed many good friendships that have lasted a lifetime. I also interacted with noncommissioned and petty officers from the other services, as well as international noncommissioned officers, and I became further convinced that the strength of the U.S. Army was our noncommissioned officer corps.

In my opinion Army NCOs were head and shoulders above in our experiences as compared to other branches and nations, though each have their own unique roles and traditions. Part of this distinction is because of our education system, but I also felt it was due to the way commissioned officers utilized the Army NCO. Besides the creation of the volunteer army and the granting of full status for women to serve, the creation of a noncommissioned officer education and management systems—all happened during my time in the Army. In my view they are what helped create the bedrock for what was emerging as a rebirth of the professional noncommissioned officer corps. Many had lamented its loss during the Vietnam War; I saw the revival firsthand and up close, and I like to think I had a part in the changes.

I knew my time was winding down at the Sergeants Major Academy, graduation was but a few months away and I was on track to walk across the stage as a graduate. Now all that was left was to learn what was up next for me. They had a name for the day the assignments were handed out to the soon-to-be graduates: Black Friday. That was the day the assignment detailers came to deliver your next posting, and for many people it did not always go as they hoped. When I was finally handed the paper with my next posting, you could have heard the breath escaping my lungs when I saw that I was heading to Korea. I had to call Gloria and let her know that I would be coming home, but not for very long.

February 15, 1987

Soldiers call it the Turtle Farm. Many who have served in South Korea know it well. Located on Camp Casey near Seoul, the Turtle Farm hosts both the in-processing and out-processing centers for soldiers bound for the 2nd Infantry Division. I started earlier in Younson and they shipped me to Casey where I learned that it earned its nickname because it usually takes a one-year tour to go from one building to the other—what soldiers say is a turtle's pace.

I had landed at Seoul and after gathering my things made my way over to the reception unit. I was getting oriented to the area and operations flow when the noncom walking me around told me that his unit there was going to need a new first sergeant. I thought, hey this could be great—I get to stay here in Seoul. I figured I would be set. Well, that thought didn't last long. When he asked me again what my last name was, and I told him Tilley, he said, "Oh, they have been calling for you at Camp Casey." Which is how I found myself at the Turtle Farm instead of basking in the good life in Seoul.

The battalion CSM met me after I arrived at Camp Casey, telling me that he had two openings for a first sergeant: one in his headquarters company and the other in a line company. Because I was a recent sergeants major course graduate looking for a new home, the CSM wanted me to consider the larger but mostly administrative headquarters company. But I figured this was likely my last chance to be a first sergeant so I selected the line. The old phrase "Be careful what you wish for, you just might get it" never even crossed my mind.

I was now on my way to Company C of the 1st Battalion, 72nd Armor, "First Tank!" Ours was the tank battalion for 1st Brigade, 2nd Infantry Division, which was the sole U.S. Army division remaining in Korea. The division was the most forward-deployed unit in the Army that was not actually in direct combat. The 2nd ID was known by many as a "trip wire" force, tasked with slowing the North Korean advance if conflict would flare-up. There had yet to be a formal peace agreement ending hostilities following the Korean War—just an armistice agreement signed between the parties.

Looking back on that assignment, I still believe it was one of my best. I had what was in my mind one of the greatest jobs a soldier can have: I was leading a company formation as the first sergeant in a place where we literally could be in conflict at any time. Yet when I arrived to Company C the unit was in shambles. The previous first sergeant had been relieved; he was an alcoholic who refused to let Army duties get in the way of his drinking. My new company had as a commander a good man who was convinced he was on the verge of being relieved, as well as a sergeant first class who was designated the interim first sergeant. I asked him to brief me on the current situation and what was going on in the company; he shrugged and explained he had just gotten there himself only a few days earlier, and he didn't know much of anything. He helped me locate where I would be staying at the senior NCO barracks and I zonked out as the jet lag set it.

The next morning was Saturday, a work day in Korea, and I went to the orderly room where there was a unit meeting going on. I walked up to the company commander and introduced myself and said "Hey sir, I am 1st Sergeant Jack Tilley, starting Monday I am going to be here as your new first sergeant and I look forward to working with you." We talked for a few a minutes before I left to settle myself in.

I spent that Sunday setting up my "hooch" and getting my things unpacked and prepared. Just as I told the commander I would, on Monday morning I stood in front of the company area and ordered the troops to fall in. I held formation and led the soldiers in PT. From that point on things began to click. The unit was filled with good people; they were motivated, and that motivated me. Because of the typical one-year assignment cycle, units like ours underwent a high amount of turnover and seeing soldiers come and go was a regular occurrence we had to deal with.

The unit went on to show good marks in many areas. We fired high tank at gunnery, our PT program was one of the top during the annual Inspector General inspection, and we would nail chemical defense drills. Korea and the 2nd Infantry Division was a great place for soldiers to train and it wasn't lost on us that we were just twenty kilometers away from the Demilitarized Zone (DMZ). That, and my competitive nature would cause me to always push my guys a little harder, and my commander could not have been happier with how the company was performing. I told him all you've got to do is plan: tell me your intention for the company, and I will make it happen for you.

One of the first things I saw that I had to do was get the company training room in order. It was so much the heart and soul of the company. It was where we deliberated and where the company leaders helped the CO plan. Our standardized procedures were outdated, and I once again found myself rewriting critical documents just as I had done with the BNCOC lessons at Fort Knox. We had alerts just like when I was in Germany, and the speed with which we went from notification to being combat ready was an important deal during an alert when you were that close to the border.

I noticed on our first load-out that once the alert signal was given, one of the few cargo trucks we had would drive to the supply room so the company could load up all its gear and go. I met with the commander and the supply sergeant and told them that I wanted the supply truck to first load up the crew-served weapons instead of making the crews individually come to the arms room. They would then drive all the weapons to where the tanks were getting ready in the motor pool. We implemented the idea the next chance we had, and we were loaded and ready to go forty-five minutes ahead of the other companies. I headed over to the chow hall to get some breakfast when the battalion commander came over to me. He said, "Hey first sergeant, what's happening? Are you going to get your company together?" I told him we were done and that I was going to go ahead and eat—unless he wanted Charlie Company to help some of the other companies? He wanted to see it for himself so he went outside to survey the battalion's progress.

I always bragged on my guys and those around me took it with a grain of salt. I would goad my fellow first sergeants to challenge Charlie Company and whenever I got around the brass I would good-naturedly encourage them to come out and experience physical fitness training (PT) with us. After hearing me brag one time too often, the division commander, Maj. Gen. Jack B. Farris, decided to come out and see for himself, and showed up unannounced at one of our PT sessions. I probably turned up the heat from my usual sessions, we must have done 150 push-ups and 150 sit-ups and ran some wind sprints before we took off on our regular five-mile route at a brisk pace. I was glad to see at the end that the general was able to hang with us the whole time, and that my troopers didn't fall out or leave a bunch of stragglers behind. After the cool down the CG said, "I want to see you first sergeant," and I led him over to our orderly room. I thought I was in trouble. We were joined by the battalion commander, who had gotten wind that the commanding general was in the battalion area and made tracks over to our company. Farris looked at me and said "First sergeant, I want to tell you two things: One is that you tell that platoon sergeant to quit chewing out those lieutenants when they don't do those push-ups very well." I gulped and said "Roger that sir." Then he said "and don't worry." I was a bit confused and asked, "Don't worry? What do you mean sir?" The CG laughed and said, "Don't worry, I ain't ever coming back." We all had a good laugh and then headed out the door. I never did see him back for PT with us again.

Everything moves fast when you're a soldier in Korea, and before you know it a year is up. In looking back, I felt that my unit was well trained and ready, and we would have been able to do what we were asked to do very well. I imagine there were things I could have done a bit better or people I could have gotten to know more, but now my time was up and I was going home to be with Gloria and the boys. One of the benefits of going to Korea at the time was that you usually already knew what your next assignment was going to be; I was going back to Fort Knox.

The promotion list was scheduled to be released and after finishing up another successful tour as a first sergeant I felt like this could very well be my time to become a sergeant major. The Army had already selected me and sent me to the Sergeants Major Course, which was usually an indication that one had the potential to become a sergeant major and was being groomed for promotion. I was now in the primary zone for promotion, meaning I had the proper amount of experience in the Army and at my current grade. I had never been selected for promotion for any grade in the secondary zone—that was the territory for the fast movers, while I was more the sure-and-steady type.

When I got back to Kentucky John Stephens was still the post sergeant major. He had decided to send me back to the NCO Academy to be the BNCOC Chief, which would be my third job as a first sergeant. I had already served on the staff at BNCOC as the Division Chief. As the first sergeant I was more like a company commander and a commandant, all rolled in to one position. The NCO academies at that time had no officers assigned, so I was the senior enlisted person in the Combat Arms BNCOC. The NCOA also had the Drill Sergeant School, which had a Chief Instructor first sergeant, as did the Combat Service Support BNCOC. Our three units, along with the staff and operations, made up the Fort Knox NCOA/DSS. I was to be there a short period before I was selected for promotion to sergeant major. I still had plenty of time for an important lesson from John Stephens.

At the time the 19K MOS was growing as more and more units were being delivered new M1 tanks and the force was in need of high-quality junior noncommissioned officers, a need that couldn't be met by the current M60-equipped units. The Army had a reenlistment program that encouraged soldiers whose enlistment was expiring to earn a bonus if they volunteered to be retrained in a new

MOS, in this case to become M1 tankers. BNCOC students were primarily sergeants and staff sergeants, and during one particular time period we had a number of bonus recipients who were relatively new to the MOS and were failing the course because they could not qualify on the tank.

An important part of my job was to meet with failing or at-risk soldiers and talk with them to determine if they were treated fairly and had the best opportunity to succeed. In my mind this group had every chance to qualify and didn't, so I had my instructors put together "drop packets" on the ones who failed multiple times. These packets were formal documentation that had to be approved by the post sergeant major before the soldiers were dropped and sent back to their units as washouts, which very well could be a career ending action.

When I got to Stephens's office with my stack of packets, he looked at them for a few seconds and then said to me, "Jack,"—he called me Jack by now—"come in here and sit down. When you were a platoon sergeant, and somebody was not successful in what they were doing, what would you do?" I said, "Well, Sergeant Major, I would train them. I would get it done and get them a passing score." He said, "Then take these packets and get the hell out of here." Pretty simple advice that I should have been more in tune with, but here's a guy who sized up a situation and knew corrective action needed to be taken by my staff and me, not with the soldiers. His message was not lost on me. We went back and worked with all until they could properly qualify.

Understanding Tilley

> *The choice of noncommissioned officers is an object of greatest importance. The order and discipline of a Regiment depends so much upon their behavior, that too much care can not be taken in preferring none to that trust but those who by their merit and good conduct are entitled to it. Honesty, Sobriety, and a remarkable attention to every point of duty, with a neatness in their dress are indispensable requisites. A spirit to command respect and obedience from the men, to teach it, are also absolutely necessary. Nor can a sergeant or corporal be said to be qualified who does not write and read in a tolerable manner.*
>
> — Baron Friedrich Wilhelm von Steuben,
> *Regulations for the Order and Discipline of the Troops of the United States*

Just because you went to the Sergeants Major Academy doesn't mean you're going to be a good sergeant major. Granted, you may have demonstrated the potential to become a sergeant major in your chosen field because you likely mastered the qualities that were expected of a future Army leader. The staff and faculty at the Sergeants Major Academy help fine-tune leaders by providing them insight and information. Students are brought to a deeper level of understanding and the curriculum offers them currency in contemporary and emerging doctrine. I was never an honor graduate from an Army school, and with one exception I was always promoted in the primary zone. And that never stopped me from reaching the pinnacle assignment for enlisted Soldiers.

At "The Academy," enlisted leaders are taught how to perform at higher levels of responsibility, as well as how to better operate above the company, troop, and battery level. One way to enhance your success rate and to become a great sergeant major is that you must be mentally and physically prepared to go through a challenging education program like the sergeants major course. And you do that not by beginning the preparation process once you learn of your selection, but earlier. Leaders must dedicate themselves to always learning and growing, as well as being students of themselves. NCOs need to possess critical thinking skills and they must be developed early; you should not wait until you need it to expose yourself to a broader desire and capacity to learn.

I understood that relationships between the company commander and the first sergeant are critical for the success of unit, and that includes all elements of company operations. There is no "NCO Business," it is all "Army Business." Noncommissioned officers must educate their superiors on all aspects of what NCOs do, including our development process and how we mentor, as well as promotion boards both locally and at the departmental level. I don't have all the right answers to ensure successful assignments in tough and demanding positions, but I am smart enough to realize that other people around me may, so I try to be smart enough to listen. I believe that success is a group effort. No one is successful by themselves, so forming and utilizing the talents of my team were always first and foremost in my mind.

[9]

COHORT

A good CSM is one that has the respect of both officers and enlisted soldiers. I also believe a good CSM is one who knows training and has the ability to mentor and motivate soldiers to do their best at everything they do. Jack Tilley was such a CSM. Both officers and enlisted alike sought his counsel. He was Master Gunner qualified, a tactician and a great confidant. He and I shared command of the battalion and we discussed important decisions and became lifelong friends.

—Lt. Col. Marion Owens, U.S. Army, Retired
former Commander, 1st Sqd, 10th Cav. Regt.

June 21, 1988

I was selected for promotion to pay grade E-9 and concurrently selected for assignment as a command sergeant major in early 1988. After a few months on the promotion list my sequence number was selected and I was assigned to the storied 1st Battalion, 10th Cavalry Regiment of the 194th Armor Brigade at Fort Knox. Formed as one of the original "Buffalo Soldier" regiments in 1866, the 1/10 Cav. was an armor battalion equipped with the M1 Abrams tank. Being a new battalion sergeant major was not going to be anything unusual for me; I understood what it took to be a good sergeant major. I figured that if you were a good tank commander, a good platoon sergeant, and a good first sergeant, then you are good. You were destined to be a good sergeant major. Up to this point the Army had given me opportunities to gain knowledge through my various assignments and schools, all designed to prepare me for this role. I was motivated and ready to go.

The 10th Cavalry was a COHORT (cohesion, operational readiness, and training) battalion. COHORT units marked a return to the bygone era of assignment policies in which soldiers would "stay with their regiment." A group of soldiers would be assigned and reassigned as a cohesive company-sized unit instead of following the individual replacement system then in use. The Army would later reinstitute portions of this concept called "modularity" as it formed "units of action" and instituted "life-cycle" unit manning to support military operations as a result of attacks in the United States on September 11, 2001.

The COHORT concept began in 1984 with the 7th Infantry Division (Light) in Fort Ord, California, as a test. That summer and fall the Army recruited and began training the soldiers under the COHORT "option," which most enlistees were not even aware of. To them it guaranteed three years in the same unit. Stationed at Fort Ord after graduation from OSUT, the 7th ID battalions were soon filled with soldiers and leaders who trained and stayed together throughout their enlistment. It was envisioned that at the twelve-month mark after the cohort's initial training was completed that the unit would rotate overseas for two years, and be replaced by another COHORT unit. At the end of that cycle the soldiers would either leave the Army or go on to become cadre to fill out the next COHORT unit, which eventually became how TF 1-10 came to exist. Around the time I arrived to 1/10 Cav. the Army had decided to continue and expand the COHORT concept, which it mostly did, although it discontinued the program in the mid-1990s.

Being a battalion sergeant major was another milestone in my career. As time went on I developed a battle rhythm that worked well for me, and I used it through many of my assignments before and after the 1/10 Cav. I would start my morning by participating in unit PT with my soldiers and then I would shower at the gym. I would have breakfast in the dining facility and then go to the office by 0800 to have a short meeting with the old man to talk about what we were going to do for the day. I served with two great battalion commanders but it was with Lt. Col. Marion Owens that I served longest. I'd go in and do paperwork or anything I had to do in the office, and then I would be out by 0930 and head down to the motor pool or check training and see what was going on within the unit. By about 1200, I would go back to the office to see what was going on and grab a bite to eat. I would head back to the office at 1300 and then walk through the battalion area to check training.

I felt that the dining facility was a great place to be with soldiers; it afforded me a lot of opportunity to connect with what was going on in the unit, and with my soldiers. One benefit besides sitting down with soldiers was that I got to talk to the first sergeants as well. They began to realize that they could find me there—I wasn't one to hang out in the office any longer that I needed to. Plus, soldiers could see me meeting with other NCOs and knew that we talked and shared information. I got a chance to do those things in the soldiers' environment and to learn about their issues. I always thought it was important to do those things because soldiers were a lot more at ease when you are talking with them in their environment. Just like when I was a first sergeant, on Saturdays and Sundays I would normally go to the barracks and visit, or walk through the battalion and talk to soldiers. It was a good habit I tried not to lose.

In becoming a command sergeant major I did not believe that my job as a noncommissioned officer had changed much; the tactics and procedures that you deal with change a little, but NCO responsibilities are basically the same no matter where you go. It's still about taking care of soldiers and making sure that the basic fundamentals are in order and focused in the right direction, and then being out with soldiers spot-checking and encouraging them to perform to their highest levels. Earlier in my career I thought I did a pretty good job, but it wasn't until later when I really started looking at things like the military planning process and understanding all the things that lead up to the execution of a task.

I began to understand my commanders' near-term and long-range goals and it allowed me to help them focus on what the training needs were for our soldiers. As the CSM I knew my role was to assist the noncommissioned officer support channel in the preparation and conduct of individual and crew training. Commanders set the plan and have a good understanding about where they want training to go; it is important that sergeants have that same understanding, and to execute their intent. It required mental focus on what our developmental processes were and was something that I took very seriously.

I was having a great time in the 10th Cavalry, one of the few deployable units on Fort Knox. The battalion had just returned from desert training at Fort Irwin, CA before I arrived and later in my tour we would be training for another exercise. Fort Knox was a good post for gunneries, which we did many, but for the wide-open spaces required to maneuver we needed to go elsewhere. Because of that we would spend time firing and maneuvering at Fort Bliss and nearby McGregor Range complex. After about eighteen months I got word that my brigade commander, Col. Don Smith, had asked the post sergeant major for a few names to consider as a replacement for his soon-to-be leaving CSM and he offered mine.

Smith cornered me one day on a break during a quarterly training briefing and asked me if I was interested in being his brigade CSM. I was concerned because I wasn't the most senior CSM on Fort Knox, but Smith only wanted to know if I was interested, so I told him I was. I was one of the candidates who had an opportunity to meet with him in something not unlike a job interview. Though as my brigade commander he knew much about me already, in the interview he asked questions about how I saw the unit going forward and what my priorities would be. I must have said some things he liked because after he finished his interviews he called me up to say, "Congratulations Sgt. Maj. Tilley, I have selected you to be my next brigade sergeant major."

February 1, 1990

The almost six thousand–soldier strong 194th Separate Armored Brigade was a bit of an anomaly. The Army in the early 1960s needed separate brigades for unique missions not appropriate to a division, so initially five Infantry brigades were created and the 16th Armor Group at Fort Ord was reflagged as the 194th Armored Brigade. After reorganization and movement to Fort Knox, the brigade's two primary roles were combat mission support for the XVIII Corps (Airborne) out of Fort Bragg, North Carolina, and an on-again, off-again role as a support unit for the Armor School. In 1989 the Army went through a major redesign in force structure as a result of new equipment and doctrine, as well as organizational redesign of tactical units. Because of that the 194th was cut to a 1,068-man, armor-heavy task force that consisted of a headquarters company, three armor companies, two mechanized infantry companies, a reserve component armor company, a field artillery battery, a supply and transport company, and a support battalion. These changes were ongoing, and by September 1990 the Army had removed one of only two deployable heavy separate brigades it had remaining in the United States.

At Fort Knox we did a lot of tank gunnery, especially with the COHORT units. For qualification, tank units like ours followed a series of twelve gunnery exercises that were sequentially harder and more sophisticated as they went along. They were listed in the gunnery manuals in tables, which is how they were described: Tables I through XII. Table I taught the individual crewmembers basic gunnery skills, which included target acquisition, target designation, gun laying, manipulation, and direct-fire adjustment. The highest level, Table XII, was a platoon-level advanced qualification course that tested a platoon's ability to engage moving and stationary targets with all tank weapons in day and night situations. In the 194th we spent a lot of time working our units through the tables, and at the brigade we helped resource the units to stay proficient.

Another tool we used to keep our crews proficient was a training device called the Unit Conduct of Fire Trainer (UCOFT). I had a particular affinity for the UCOFT. When I was with the team creating the first 19K OSUT, the 1st AIT/ OSUT brigade commander, Col. Andrew P. O'Meara, had me travel with him to Florida to look at a UCOFT prototype and to serve as a tank gunner for his exploratory visit. The

UCOFT was basically a tank simulator in a large metal container that allowed a crew to work at functional mock-up stations that looked and felt like the interior of the M1 tank. After we had gone through a few exercises replicating how a tank crew would perform, O'Meara asked me what I thought about it. I told him that if the Army buys these things that it is going to be a game changer and raise the level of training in units; in the end they did buy them, and delivered a number of the devices to the 1st Training Brigade.

When the 194th was converted to a combined arms task force with its small number of active army support units, it was planned that we were to be aligned with reserve component units who would "round out" our structure and join us should we deploy. Unfortunately, world events would not wait: In August 1990 Iraqi leader Saddam Hussein ordered his military to invade Kuwait, kicking off a showdown between Iraq and a broad international coalition. As the United States and its partners drew a "line in the sand," the U.S. military began moving forces to Saudi Arabia as part of Desert Shield. Because of the post–Cold War troop reductions and the fact that we had not yet been filled with our round-out partners, Col. Smith and I knew the likelihood of the 194th deploying as an armored brigade was slim. Our personnel were instead used to fill out critical troop shortages in CONUS-based III Corps units that were deploying to Saudi Arabia, ensuring that those units went overseas with 100 percent of their authorized strength. We were destined to watch the events of Desert Shield and later Desert Storm unfold on our televisions.

Soon after the Gulf War ended the command sergeant major of the 1st Armored Division was selected to go to the III Corps at Fort Hood, and my nomination by Smith was put forward by Stephens for consideration as his replacement. At the time it took a brigade-level commander or higher to nominate a serving command sergeant major. This ensured candidates were qualified to compete based on the vacancy announcement that went out to the senior sergeants major, those in "nominative" positions who served a general officer. As the post command sergeant major, Stephens's role was to ensure I was in fact ready for the increased responsibilities of the job. I was pleased to learn that I was selected as one of the finalists for the position. After the announcements were made I and the other candidates were flown to Germany to meet with the commanding general, Maj. Gen. William Boice.

When we got to Germany we received a briefing on the division and its current activities and on the second day we each went through a personal interview with the division commander. Actually, I had two interviews; the second time I went in to see him he thought I was more than qualified for the job, but he was a family man as well and asked if our family was up for the assignment because of Brian. He was concerned that my son might not get the care he needed, that was the kind of man he was. We were by now enrolled in the Army's Exceptional Family Member Program, so we were given assignment limitations because of Brian's condition.

Boice looked me in the eye and asked, "Are you really sure that you want this kind of job because of the commitment it puts on you and your family?" I thought about that for a moment and told him, "If I didn't think we could sir, I wouldn't be here right now." After he dismissed me it was about fifteen minutes before he came out and told all the candidates that we "did a great job, but I've selected CSM Tilley to be my division sergeant major." Everybody shook my hand and about three minutes later there was nobody left in the room, and so I went back into the general's office. I said, "Hey, sir, I've never been a division sergeant major before, can you tell me what you want me to do?" Boice smiled and said "Yes, can you go home, get your stuff, and come on back as quickly as you can?" So, I made my way back to Kentucky to collect Gloria and the boys and we eventually set our course for Germany again.

March 16, 1992

The Army in Europe had changed since my first assignment in 1976. By this time, it had been just a little over six years since the Berlin Wall had been chipped away by throngs of celebratory Germans. I had the privilege of serving as the command sergeant major for one of the two U.S. divisions remaining in Europe, the 1st Armored Division. It was nicknamed "Old Ironsides" by its first commander, Maj. Gen. Bruce R. Magruder, after the frigate USS *Constitution*. The division had a historic legacy as the first armored division to see combat in World War II. At the conclusion of the war the division was deactivated until the Korean War broke out. Though not deployed to Korea or Vietnam, its soldiers and equipment served as the nucleus for the creation of the U.S. Constabulary and as a test bed for armored divisions for the "Atomic Field Army," and the division was deployed as part of the U.S. buildup for a potential invasion during the Cuban missile crisis of 1962. The 1st Armored Division relocated in 1971 to Ansbach, West Germany, where it served until its deployment to the Middle East in support of Operation Desert Storm. It returned from the Middle East in May 1991 and moved to Rose Barracks in Bad Kreuznach at the former 8th Infantry Division headquarters.

Being a division sergeant major wasn't much different in my eyes than being a command sergeant major at other levels. My duties and responsibilities were mainly influenced by my experience and span of control. I still saw myself in a similar role that I performed at the battalion and brigade; the 1st AD was just larger and more geographically dispersed. We had many small camps, called "kasernes," that were located at various points in our region. One of the major differences between what I did at Fort Knox and what I did in Germany was that I had to drive longer distances to get out to see my soldiers, which often made for early mornings and late nights.

To keep my routine, I had to get up at 0300 on many a morning so I could make it to the various unit locations in time to participate in physical training. It seemed no matter the direction I would have to travel an hour or an hour and a half to get to any location. To ensure I was splitting my time accurately, I devised a checklist that had all the units on it and I would mark the dates when I would visit each one. That way I knew whether or not I was missing a certain unit or giving another too much of my time. It was a system that worked well for me and allowed me to keep in tune with how often I needed to travel so I could balance it with my required duties back at the division headquarters.

Just like in my earlier assignments, I felt that my role at the division was to help others succeed, whether it was noncommissioned officers or commissioned officers. As the division CSM, I would often visit units and come across something that did not seem right. I would sometimes have to take issues to commanders, which can be a sensitive topic.

If I found a standard not being met or an activity that didn't seem right and the sergeant major or support channel couldn't fix it, I would take it to the chain of command.

I was never the kind of leader to say "Look, I'm the division sergeant major and you're going to do this and this," but I saw it as my role to coach and advise. So, after I shared my thoughts based on my experience, which usually was laced pretty heavily with my CG's intent or Army policy, if a commander or leader did not want to comply, my best strategy was to say "Hey, look, if you're going to do that, I feel obligated to discuss this with the division commander." In most cases it allowed me to catch the leader's attention, and many times it broke the stalemate.

I loved being with the leaders and general officers of the division; it was truly a highlight of my military career. After having worked together for many months I remember asking Gen. Boice if he would mind if I "promoted" him into the ranks of the noncommissioned officer. He said sure, and I asked him what rank he would prefer. He said he wanted to be a sergeant (E-5), so I had the staff draw up a ceremony. We had orders published and had everything in place to formalize the event, so as the presiding NCO I called him forward to receive his honorary rank. After I pinned the stripes on his collar we afforded him time to speak. He stood in front of the small audience and began to tear up as he explained the significance of the milestone, and he thanked me for doing this.

Afterwards I was asked by many people why the general seemed so emotional about this mostly ceremonious act, so I recounted a story the general had once told me: When Boice was on the staff at West Point (he was Class of 1963) he was as proud as he could be right after he had been promoted to major. When he had got home later that day he told his young son of his accomplishment and explained he had just been promoted. The son was impressed but wanted to know, "When are you going to be promoted to sergeant?" Unfortunately, that son could not be there to witness me pinning on his father the stripes of a sergeant because tragically he had been killed years before by a drunk driver.

When serving at successive levels of increased responsibility, one occasionally comes in conflict with others. I felt I was an easygoing leader who took his job seriously, but I would challenge soldiers in positive ways. However, when those methods didn't work—and they sometimes didn't—I had no problems adjusting my approach to become a more of an authoritarian or disciplinarian. It was a part of the style that I created as a young sergeant, and it matured as I came to better understand what motivates soldiers. I believe it was proven through the successes of my soldiers and their units. I could say I was never in a "bad" unit, and that most of the people who I soldiered with were great Americans. In my more than five years as a division sergeant major, there were only three or four soldiers I had a run-in with; two of those incidents were related to medical problems and the actions that I felt needed to be taken.

I also had to deal with my own peers, as not all division sergeants major had the same view of how to run an organization, which was fine with me. The role of the command sergeant major in my eyes was to be the honest broker who can tell it like it is. It's the capacity for providing commanders the unvarnished truth without the fear of reprisal that makes the position of a command sergeant major so valuable. But it is the mark of the great ones who can do that with dignity and respect, while still maintaining the good order and discipline of an organization that supports the formal chain of command.

It was much tougher to mentor and coach NCO leaders I didn't see that often. I focused two levels down, on brigade and battalion sergeants major, so I had to work at ways for us to connect at work and in play. It was a challenge that Boice had to deal with as well with his commanders, so we would hold regular events quarterly. We would have luncheons to bring senior NCOs together or the general would host functions for the command teams; we had a number of ways to build teams. When it came to individuals, I would use my knack for sports and competition: I would run or play racquetball with the sergeants major of the division when I could, or take them golfing. I had started playing golf at Fort Knox and enjoyed the game, and spending time on the course with a couple of NCOs was one way to get us talking openly. It was a great way for mentoring and counseling a leader in a nonthreatening way, like how I did with soldiers in the mess halls of Fort Knox.

As I became more senior, so did those I was charged to oversee, so my techniques had to change. Not everyone enjoyed golf, so I would look for a connection between us. Bored soldiers like to play a card game called Spades, so if that was the game to get us to connect, then deal me in. For someone else it may have been coffee or a 7-Up. Whatever it was I would give it a shot if it would put me on their level to get them to open up. At every level, communication was the way I could understand what the successes and challenges were. I could better understand the issues and take them back to division to support the soldiers. That is what I felt sergeants major were best at—that, and taking care of soldiers and their families. In my view, taking care of people is knowing them, counseling them, and making sure that they're professionally developed for the next level, which is what soldiers expect from their leaders.

Understanding Tilley

> *The NCO support channel (leadership chain) parallels and complements the chain of command. It is a channel of communication and supervision from the command sergeant major to first sergeant and then to other NCOs and enlisted personnel of the units. Commanders will define responsibilities and authority of their NCOs to their staffs and subordinates.*
> —Noncommissioned officer support channel,
> *AR 600-20, Army Command Policy*

There must be a clear understanding between the CSM and the commander on what exactly your roles are within that unit, and this is true for any position or assignment within the noncommissioned officer support channel. When you assume your position, you have to sit down early with your commander and look him or her in the eye and ask, "What is it that you want the command sergeant major to focus on," and then be prepared to accept your commander's guidance. Some of the roles or specified tasks are time-honored and well understood, but much is left open to a commander's prerogative, so this type of conversation helps clear up any ambiguity regarding roles and responsibilities.

I believe a commander should challenge his or her command sergeants major to be visible and out mingling with soldiers. Battlefield circulation is nothing more than leadership by walking around. You also must be the honest broker for the commander, telling him or her your impressions about what you see. The relationship between the commander and the senior NCO includes the directed tasks like managing the enlisted development process, mentorship, promotions and selection boards, evaluations and awards, and all the day-to-day operations that it takes to keep the organization moving forward. But it is in the realm of the more contemporary challenges and emerging requirements that there could be confusion. This type of direction and expectation is empowerment, and often is very personal or unit or commander specific. It is where you each openly discuss the CSM's specific functions and boundaries as the senior enlisted advisor, and it lays the foundation for creating trust and building the command team. It is also your initial counseling session, and it should be done privately with your commander.

I generally knew what my role was. When I was a platoon sergeant my responsibility was to take care of that platoon and when I was a first sergeant my job was to take care of that company. And as a division command sergeant major I knew that my role was to take care of all those brigades and battalions. Looking back, it is difficult to say which one or two things were most important for the command sergeant major to focus on, because I don't think there is just one. It is important that once your commander has empowered you that he or she transmits those roles to their subordinate commanders at least two levels down so they are also aware of how your commander intends to use you. This is true for all positions within the noncommissioned officer support channel.

[10]

IFOR

In preparation for our deployment to Bosnia I challenged the soldiers of Task Force Eagle to always display the characteristics of a tough, disciplined, competent and professional military force and no one maintained that standard more than Jack Tilley. His personal example, leadership, support, and friendship were critical to not only our success, but to my sanity.

—Maj. Gen. William L. Nash, U.S. Army, Retired
former Commander, 1st Armored Division
and Task Force Eagle

December 2, 1995

It was a typically cold December day in Germany. My driver, Sgt. Roger Gomez, was fighting the Saturday traffic in an effort to beat my now-boss Maj. Gen. Bill Nash and other VIP's to Smith Barracks in Baumholder, Germany, the home of over 4,000 combat soldiers and the headquarters of the 2nd Brigade, 1st Armored Division. Once we arrived at the gates I saw a smattering of protestors, one with a sign that read "Draft Dodger Go Home." I soon found out that fog had grounded the commanding general's helicopter, so he and the rest of the entourage would travel to the barracks by motorcade once the President of the United States, Bill Clinton, had finished meeting with German chancellor Helmut Kohl.

Our sitting President, code-name POTUS (President Of The United States), was on the way to address the Supreme

Allied Command's chosen representatives of the United States military, the 1st Armored Division, and soldiers of the division were to be his backdrop. American service men and women had traveled far and wide to come to Baumholder to possibly catch a glimpse of the president and hear his speech.

We knew already what he was about to tell us. The division had been preparing on and off for three years to be ready to separate the factions in the war-torn former Yugoslav republics; the latest hot spot was Bosnia-Herzegovina. The warring parties had agreed to a shaky cease-fire while a peace plan was being hammered out by international diplomats, and we were intent on hearing the results because we had expected to be called in to action as the U.S. response force should the president authorize the commitment of American forces. For many in the crowd at Smith Barracks that morning, this was not to be a Christmas greeting well received.

The conflicts in the former Yugoslavia had been on our minds since the moment I returned to Germany. After the Berlin Wall came down in November 1989, the breakup of the Soviet Union led to turmoil in the eastern European countries. One casualty was Yugoslavia, a socialist country that had not aligned with either power during and after World War II. It had been led by emperor for life Josip Tito, whose death in 1980 marked the beginning of a more than ten-year decline in the country's fortunes. Yugoslavia experienced a fracture that coincided with the fall of the wall as some of its republics declared independence. Bitter fighting and ethnic cleansing broke out in Slovenia and Croatia, which required the United Nations (UN) to step in an attempt to curb the violence.

American forces had been watching all of this unfold with a wary eye. The division had been designated as the American response force should the UN or the National Atlantic Treaty Organization (NATO) require assistance. As early as May 1992 we were a part of the planning efforts of the U.S. Army Europe (USAREUR) and the V Corps staffs as different courses of action and operational plans were being discussed; we had more than a few false starts, with orders to pack and go each time there was a flare-up in the region. The U.S. Army had been providing peacekeepers in the Republic of Macedonia since 1992 and our division sent its first rotational unit in December 1994. As fighting in the republics got heavier in mid-1995 our planning began to consider that we might have to be a go-between for belligerents, and the October cease-fire was a signal to the staff that we may finally receive that call. Though there was skepticism that we would deploy, we had long been planning to do so. To help us prepare USAREUR had conducted two planning and training exercises called Mountain Eagle that focused on our abilities to deploy. Meanwhile we waited for peace accords being held in Dayton, Ohio, to conclude.

I was about to leave the headquarters the night before we were alerted when the buzz going around the building was that we were sure to receive deployment orders at any moment. Though I was in tune with the latest intelligence and had been watching the news I had a nagging feeling that we had been down this road before. I told one of the soldiers on the command group staff, "Yeah, right. If something happens call me at home," and I left for the night. Imagine my surprise when I came in the next morning to find everybody running around; it appeared to me that they were executing our standing alert procedures to notify the division in the event of a warning of hostilities. I asked what the hell was going on, and one of the staffers told me "We've been alerted. We're moving out." I asked why they didn't have someone call me and was told, "We didn't want to bother you." Well hell, we were just about to embark on a major deployment as one of the largest operations in Europe for the United States since World War II and somebody didn't want to inconvenience the division sergeant major.

We had advance notice that President Clinton would be coming to Germany to make his speech, and his choosing a location in the 1st Armored Division area made good sense. Baumholder was selected because of its size and location, and it was home to a great brigade with a wonderful command team. Because of fog the German chancellor rode to Baumholder with the president, and once they arrived it was show time. During the delay I went to the podium and grabbed the microphone to give the troops a pep talk and we practiced shouting our best "HOOAH" cheer for when the president would arrive.

When his motorcade arrived, he was met by Gen. George Joulwan, the Supreme Allied Commander, Europe and my boss Maj. Gen. Nash. I had the thrill of being able to join the group to escort the president, and we would continue to see him, Mrs. Clinton, and their daughter Chelsea, along with many other dignitaries, in the days and weeks to come. At a later visit of his to our camp in Bosnia I was asked to introduce the president to the crowd. I stood in front of all who were there, mostly the soldiers of the division and our task force, and said "Ladies and Gentlemen, the President of the United States." That was the first and only time I ever got to say that.

*Men and women of Task Force Eagle, I know the burden
of our country's leadership now weighs most heavily
on you and your families. Each and every one of you
who have volunteered to serve this country makes hard
sacrifices. We send you a long way from home for a long
time. We take you away from your children and your
loved ones. These are the burdens that you assume for
America, to stand up for our values, to serve our interests,
to keep our country strong in this time of challenge and
change.*

— President William J. Clinton,
Speech excerpt, December 2nd, 1995

On December 17 our Division Assault Command Post,
led by Assistant Division Commander Brig. Gen. Stan
Cherrie, arrived in Sarajevo to begin our deployment efforts
and to prepare to receive the U.S. ground contingent to the
NATO peacekeeping operation dubbed Operation Joint
Endeavor. I figured we were going to have to fight our way
in. We were to be part of a multinational peacekeeping force
known as the NATO Implementation Force (IFOR). The
NATO forces were there to assume peacekeeping duties from
the UN force, which had been in the region since 1992, and
the general and I were to take part in a transfer of authority
between the UN and NATO by December 20, 1995.

As soldiers and equipment loaded up for their rail journey
to a staging base in Hungary, Army engineers were fighting
the Sava River in an effort to temporarily replace the bridges
felled during the war. The river was Yugoslavia's longest, and
it had swelled due to recent weather. Our attempts to connect
Croatia and Bosnia via a float bridge were obstructed. The

Sava became even more of a problem when a few days later the engineers' base camp was flooded when the river crested. It would not be until December 31 that the bridge was complete and the tanks of the 1/1 Cav. Regt. rolled in to Bosnia. Task Force Eagle, the name given to the 1st Armored Division as the U.S. ground contingent, had arrived.

The division was slated to establish Task Force Eagle in the Multinational Division-North (MND-N), one of three NATO multinational divisions. Located in Tuzla, Bosnia-Herzegovina, MND-N was composed of two U.S. brigades, a Russian brigade, a Turkish brigade, and the Nordic-Polish Brigade. Before we left the Nash pulled together the brigade commanders and told them they need to be prepared to fight. The next day he and I flew in with a portion of the Main Command Post to Tuzla two days in advance of the transfer of authority in order to prepare. We would spend Christmas in Bosnia-Herzegovina with what would become a force of 60,000 strong. After a brief ceremony we made the change official by lowering a sign indicating the UN mission and replaced it with a Task Force Eagle sign, signifying the camp and all it stood for was now under NATO control.

It was just Nash and I, plus a small contingent of Americans who were in Bosnia at this point; our main concern was ensuring the rest of Task Force Eagle got into the country safely. The general was my third commanding officer since I had been with the division, he had been on board since June and we had formed a great bond by now. I understood the burden placed upon him, the world's eyes were on all that we did. Though the politicians were touting our operation as peacekeeping, Nash was wary. Earlier he had noted in the *Field Artillery* magazine that "A peacekeeping mission can quickly escalate into one of peacemaking, peace enforcement or some other current phrase that means soldiers on the scene are involved in close combat."

Our initial battle rhythm after the transfer of authority was that the general and I would fly south by helicopter to the Sava River and check out the progress the engineers were making, and then we would head up to Tuzla so he could attend meetings and delegation visits. I would then load up my guys in my Humvee and head back south by road. I would visit with soldiers and then make my way north again ready to repeat the cycle. After the bridge was finally built and the division got into place I believe we had thirty-seven remote camps and sites and 13,000 soldiers—and it was my goal to get out and see as many soldiers as I could at every site.

My Vietnam tour had prepared me for the nature of an operation such as Operation Joint Endeavor. The country had been in the midst of conflict and strife just weeks earlier, and we were now standing between opposing forces in something that was being called "peace enforcement." I was a soldier, not a politician, so I only paid enough attention to the rhetoric back in Washington to stay abreast of the situation. My goal was to make sure we were prepared for what might come at us. One of our initial concerns was the high number of land mines that had been spread over the country: reports of the time claimed that they numbered in the millions. And because many of the minefields were not placed there by professional soldiers who understood the need, maps or records were few and far between—meaning a high number of the mines were not accounted for.

Because of this, during our preparation we spent a great amount of time teaching individuals within the division on the ways to deal with the mine threat. Before a soldier could deploy he or she had to go through set "lanes" scenarios, including reacting to mines, marking a minefield, first aid, and weapons qualification. We had a few months to prepare ourselves because of the pace of the peace accords, which allowed us the luxury of time.

It wasn't too long into the operation that I noticed key leaders and the staff were working themselves at a hectic pace. I continuously had to remind people we were in it for a year—this was not like a trip to the field or a gunnery, and so setting up a battle rhythm and developing a sleep plan was critical. I traveled almost 60,000 miles in my "Humvee" to get out and be among the soldiers and leaders of the division. There was never a day off for the soldiers of Task Force Eagle, but we tried to set up "down days" when units could allow for it, and I was a strong advocate for unit sports. I also found myself consulting with leaders about the importance of sharing and delegating some of their tasks. We had great noncommissioned officers and soldiers in the staffs and they could shoulder some of the burdens the leaders had. I would remind them the soldiers in their sections could prepare reports and do some of the routine tasks and that they did not have to do everything. They should make sure to use all the people within their organization.

As the weeks and months wore on I began to worry most about complacency. As the senior noncommissioned officer, the commanding general had tasked me with focusing on standards and ensuring that first-line leaders were enforcing them. Nash was a hard but fair armored cavalryman, a Silver Star recipient who was known to cuss with the best of them and had a love for a good cigar. He once told me, "I don't care if people call you a mean son of a bitch, as long as you are enforcing standards and discipline." He and I had a great relationship and we remain friends even in our post-military careers.

In an operation like this one the major responsibility for each soldier was to properly accomplish the basic fundamentals of soldiering. That means tasks like keeping your weapons clean, wearing your uniform properly, and staying focused on what you are doing. Vietnam showed me how complacency could be a killer, and I described it that way to the soldiers when I talked about the need to remain focused. Our soldiers needed to have a sense of "situational awareness" that gave them that edge to be ready for anything.

To me situational awareness also meant planning for the unexpected and the worst-case scenarios. Static checkpoint and basecamp operations often became boring or routine, so it was up to the leaders to get out and ensure we did not let complacency infect the task force. Everywhere I went I focused on inspecting units on adherence to our published standards. That meant procedures for vehicle convoys, in wearing standardized uniforms, inspecting guard towers, or just checking what was important to that type of unit's mission. Even with that attention, we took our first casualty to a mine just over a month after crossing the Sava River: Sgt. 1st Class Donald A. Dugan was a platoon sergeant with A Troop, 1/1 Cav. who was the NCOIC of a checkpoint in Gradacac.

Another area Nash asked me to focus was the accidental or "negligent" discharge of weapons. Though it was a peace-enforcement mission we were armed with live ammunition, with many units carrying their basic combat load of individual and crew-served weapons. Early on there were concerns and misconceptions regarding overly strict Rules of Engagement or bureaucratic Escalation of Force measures. (These are published and memorized guidelines that soldiers use to determine when and if it is appropriate to respond to certain situations with deadly force.) In the end, the ROE allowed soldiers to protect themselves and their comrades, and it was never much of a problem or source of confusion during our deployment.

Because of our force-protection rules we always loaded a magazine in an individual weapon whenever we went off the camps so that should the need arise soldiers were adequately prepared to respond. Our biggest problem was in the soldiers' lack of experience or improper training; that occasionally led to bullets being discharged unintentionally from a weapon when it was jarred or dropped, or by a trigger squeeze at a "clearing" barrel. Not all discharges came from personal weapons, and it happened to too many people. Nash had directed anybody who had a negligent discharge to meet with me, and one time it was a captain. I met with him and I started off, "Sir, you know you outrank me and I know you outrank me, but you can either let me tell you why you screwed up or you can explain it to the commanding general." He agreed to handle it with me, and afterward when Nash asked me about a company officer accidently shooting his weapon I told him I had already taken care of it.

One area in which I asserted myself was in providing morale and recreation opportunities. I knew that when it was possible for soldiers to take part in fitness and sports activities it would help keep them fit as well as offer a way to relieve stress. We were told initially that our deployment would be up to a year, and so as far as I was concerned it was going to be 365 days. We had to settle in for the long haul. The Exchange was busy setting up in-country stores, and they helped provide some of the comforts soldiers wanted access to; they also hired barbers for haircuts. We had mail service and gyms, and the United Services Organization (USO) brought in talent from the United States to entertain the troops.

I had attended church on Eagle Base one Sunday and during the service I heard a young soldier sing. I remember thinking to myself how good he was, so when it was over I went over and asked if he would like to sing for the troops. He said he would love to, so I told him to get in my Humvee and he began to travel with me. Then I added more people, eventually three in total. As I would go around and meet with people I always would gather a crowd, and the singers would just blend in. I would then ask the crowd if they wanted a show, and they would usually get worked up, and then the singers would perform. They were really good—they sang country songs and would be hootin' and a hollerin'—and the soldiers loved it. I would take small groups like this with me whenever I could in order to help raise the morale of the troops. They just loved it.

We also had entertainers visit us from the United States. Sheryl Crow had been traveling with then–First Lady Hillary Clinton as part of USO-sponsored entertainment troupe, singing for the troops. She offered to go to our forward camps, so I escorted her as we headed out via helicopter to nearby Camp Lisa. I wanted to clown around with one of the sergeants major who was posted there, Cmd. Sgt. Maj. Mike Bush. He was a no-nonsense paratrooper serving as the battalion sergeant major of 3rd Battalion, 12th Infantry, and he had a ton of experience in light and airborne infantry units; he was no stranger to deployment.

I jokingly asked Crow for a favor. I pointed Bush out to her and I asked that after she got out of the helicopter to walk right up to him and kiss him and say "Hello, Mike, I haven't seen you in a long time." She laughed and good-naturedly played along with the gag, doing just that. Unaware of the joke, the strait-laced soldier was flabbergasted. He did not expect that type of greeting from such a well-known star, especially one he had never met. Of course, I was off to the side laughing, watching his confusion—his face must have changed a couple of different shades of red. I always looked-for opportunities—in the right setting—to relax and "let one's hair down." In a place like Bosnia we had to stay focused all the time, so I felt it was our role as senior NCOs to finds ways to let soldiers blow off some steam. I figured if we were wound tight all the time, so would our soldiers be.

Complacency continued to be a big concern for me, and being prepared and not taking soldier obligations for granted were high on my list. For better protection Nash mandated that no vehicles would travel outside the base camps without being in a convoy of at least three vehicles, which caused grumbling across the task force. To ensure the word was getting out I spot-checked wherever I went. I checked the weapons of thirty soldiers one day, and I was disappointed in what I saw: five would not have fired and fifteen were dirty. To me this was the failing of the noncommissioned officer supervisors who should have been ensuring that these tasks were performed; even worse was that there were a few NCOs in the group of offenders. The NCOs who had assumed their soldiers were performing their tasks without spot-checking were the leading culprits, and it was something I set out to fix.

In May we began "rest and recuperation," (R&R) leave periods, and soldiers could take a single two-week respite at some point during the expected one-year deployment. We wanted to keep our crews sharp so we worked with the MND-Southwest and set up a firing range at an abandoned military base in Glamoc. We later conducted live-fire exercises and gunneries there, which allowed our units to get in some much-needed training and practice. As the deployment dragged on through the summer, we had to worry less about cold-weather injuries and instead ensured the troops were staying hydrated and did not become heat casualties.

If people had to travel off-camp it was always in a group, and our policy was that any time a vehicle departed base camp that flak jackets, load-carrying equipment, and Kevlar helmets were to be worn at all times. If a convoy had to stop for any reason soldiers were expected to exit their vehicles and provide security. In our view, an alert crew demonstrating a positive show of force would go a long way towards dissuading aggression and presented a strong, professional image. In the end, we had very few acts of aggression towards our soldiers, and in many cases it was the opposite: many of the people of Bosnia-Herzegovina were glad that we were there.

The president had told us to expect to spend a year in Bosnia, and initially we didn't know what to expect beyond that. As time began to tick by it was clear our mission was not complete, so a follow-on force would have to come in behind us. It was decided that it was to be the other Germany-based division, the 1st Infantry Division. As we got closer to that time I asked the NCOs of the division to play close attention to two important aspects that lay ahead: the complicated risks of doing a division-wide relief in place, and the reintegration of soldiers and their families when we returned after a year separation.

We had worked hard to establish family support groups and created "rear detachment" teams of leaders who helped keep communication flowing between family groups and the units, and our Base and Area Support units did a great job in keeping the services up and running on the posts. We began reintegration training a few months before soldiers started rotating back home, and even allowed spouses to attend some classes through the support groups. As part of the redeployment soldiers were screened and saw a number of specialists who looked for unnoticed signs of stress or problems, and we offered coping techniques after reintegration.

As soldiers were returning to Germany they transitioned through the same staging base in Hungary that many went through some twelve months before, and they found it had since taken on a more entrenched, enduring presence. Our soldiers had been restricted from alcohol during their entire tour while in country; we needed people on their game twenty-four hours a day. But in Hungary they did not have that rule, and had instituted a "club" for soldiers to relax and let their hair down when they were off-duty. As we were planning to redeploy the corps commander wanted it closed and alcohol kept off-limits until our soldiers reached home. I asked the simple question: Do we want soldiers having their first beer alone and away from their leadership, or can we maybe limit the amount and allow them to have the same privileges of every other soldier on that camp? I merely suggested that we trust our soldiers and hold violators accountable for their actions. The corps CG relented and the beer tent remained open, and we hardly had a problem.

In the end it was the people of Bosnia-Herzegovina and the region who benefited the most from our presence there, and we were privileged to have been selected for that first mission. There was, and continues to be, a lot of discussion about whether we should have gone, and whether peacekeeping or peace enforcement is a role for the United

States Army. I can only say that for the value of preparing, training, and deploying a division that was able to provide some good to a troubled people on the ground, it was an honorable use of forces. Soldier, staff, and leaders all benefited from the experience. Through the constant rotations—like the other deployments before—in many ways the experience helped our Army better prepare for the continuous grind of repeated deployments that lay ahead.

Understanding Tilley

> *But we in it shall be remembered—We few, we happy few, we band of brothers;*
> *For he to-day that sheds his blood with me Shall be my brother.*
> —William Shakespeare,
> *Henry V*

You can easily identify commanders at every level that really appreciate what the command sergeant major is doing both for them and on their behalf, and Maj. Gen. Nash was one of those leaders. You could have the best general or the best colonel in the world and have a terrible sergeant major and that commander is not going have a very good command tour. But you could have a really good sergeant major and an average colonel and they are going to succeed because that sergeant major will benefit his or her commander and enable his or her success. That's really what our job is as senior noncommissioned officers: aid our leaders in being more effective.

There are many responsibilities of a command sergeant major. It is through your knowledge and talent that you achieve success. Leaders mature through a development process that often dictates how you progress coming up through the ranks. Great soldiers are often guided by mentors and leaders and by their many experiences; it is these relationships that set you up for success. The relationships formed with people who you meet in the military can last a lifetime. You might think upon meeting someone that you will never see them again, but that is not always true. You may serve together somewhere or even run into them when you get out of the military. You may work for them or with them in civilian life, or seek them out to help you find a job. So if you think slamming doors in people's faces and treating people like shit is a good thing, you are wrong. It's a bad trait for a lot of reasons, but most importantly, because you are supposed to be a professional soldier and professionals do not treat people badly.

In my first correspondence to the soldiers and noncommissioned officers of Task Force Eagle I reminded them that our top priority was accomplishment of the overall mission as described by our national command authority. For us that was treaty compliance, mission accomplishment, and force protection. And because of the political and multinational climate we were in, all three went hand-in-hand. Failure to accomplish one would have allowed only partial accomplishment of the other two.

Nash and I challenged the leaders of the division, especially the noncommissioned officers, to keep their head in the game. I was mostly concerned that as routines were formed across the division that there would be a sense of peace, and complacency would settle in. To me it was paramount that leaders keep their guard up and keep their soldiers safe. Our nation continues to commit forces to operations; each mission may be different and unique, but the time-honored principles of leadership are fundamental. America's Army is typically employed to accomplish a specific mission of national importance, and for that the value of noncommissioned officers enforcing standards and discipline will be timeless.

[11]

Area of Responsibility

Throughout an officer's career in the military he might be fortunate enough to serve with a rare senior NCO who not only works hard to make the command better, but also works hard to make you better as a leader. Jack Tilley was one of those. His advice to me on how best to apply my leadership in a command as large and diverse as CENTCOM was invaluable. He had a sixth sense about when and where I should make my presence known; who I should talk to in order to get a real sense of how things were going; and where outstanding performance should be recognized that might normally go unnoticed. His leadership was felt throughout the command.
—Gen. Anthony C. Zinni, U.S. Marine Corps, Retired,
former Commander-in-Chief,
U.S. Central Command

December 2, 1995

After five and a half years as the top noncom of the 1st Armored Division I knew it was time to move on. I had already served three commanders. A fourth, Maj. Gen. Larry Ellis, had just taken command of the division and had asked me to stay. I had already planned to leave, but I went home and told Gloria what he had asked; she told me to go back and tell him that we had already shipped our car back to the States. I felt it was time for new blood in the position, as I strongly believed that after a while you can lose sight of moving an organization forward, and I knew my time was up. I had become familiar with my role as "Iron 7" and I was enjoying the results of the programs I had supported and led, but I felt it was time that the division had a fresh perspective. Gloria and I had talked and we decided we would like to go back to Kentucky. I would have been happy to serve out another few years as the Armor School CSM at Fort Knox and start the transition from soldier to civilian. I had considered retiring there.

Gloria and I were preparing to return to the United States when Cmd. Sgt. Maj. William Morgan of the U.S. Army Space and Strategic Defense Command stopped by to visit. Morgan was retiring soon and wanted me to consider replacing him; the application window had just closed and he had hoped for a broader slate of candidates to offer his boss, Lt. Gen. Edward Anderson. I told him I was "just a tanker" and that I didn't know much about space. He laughed and told me that they had plenty of people with those specialties on the staff—what the command needed was a leader with the type of field experience that I had. I told him I would consider it.

In the meantime, I was invited to join some of the most influential sergeants major from across the Army at a workshop in El Paso, Texas, where we were to find ways to strengthen and modernize how the Army developed noncommissioned officers. The workshop was called for by the Sergeant Major of the Army Gene C. McKinney and hosted by the Training and Doctrine Command Sergeant Major James C. McKinney (who happened to be twin brothers). The sixty attendees represented all the components and included the most senior sergeants major from some of the military branches, armies, corps divisions, and NCO academies, and also included leaders from the Army National Guard and Army Reserve. This six-day event of discussion and debate included a series of talks in which representatives of the NCO corps laid out what they perceived to be the strengths and weaknesses in the professional development of noncommissioned officers, all with the help of personnel from the non-profit think tank RAND Corporation. Through the use of RAND's techniques in those working discussions the group created topics to present to the Training and Doctrine Commander to be considered for future programs of noncommissioned officer development.

After I returned to Germany I was notified that the Army Space and Strategic Defense Command slate was in fact reopened, and I was encouraged to put in my nomination packet. I applied; I always figured that if it did not work out I'd had a great run, and would be just fine moving on to Ft Knox. I was selected to interview in Arlington, VA with the commanding general. The interview went well and I felt that we had a good conversation; he asked me if I would consider accepting the job. I was about to answer him when he suggested I talk with my wife first, so I called Gloria and asked her about it. She agreed to the assignment, and I told the general I accepted. Then the realization sunk in that I again had to move—and now I had to figure out "the Beltway."

I had no illusions about the assignment. I understood that it would be much different from what I was used to. I would go from a unit comprising almost 18,000 soldiers to one of 1,100. During my tenure, the command reorganized and became the U.S. Army Space and Missile Defense Command (SMDC). Primarily located in one of the many federal buildings in the Washington, DC area, this field-operating agency served as the Army agent in matters of space and missile defense. SMDC can trace its roots back to the days before the National Aeronautics and Space Administration (NASA), it had been created during a time when the Army had led the nation's space efforts. Its predecessor is credited with building and then launching our first ballistic missile and earth-orbiting satellites, and now as one of the first command sergeants major of this newly redesignated major army command I found myself immersed in the world of honest-to-goodness rocket scientists.

The SMDC had the primary responsibility for ensuring warfighters had access to space-based resources, and the soldiers of our command had an important role in that mission. It may have at first been a little daunting for me to come to a unique command like SMDC, but I had received instructions from Anderson, and I knew and understood the role of the senior enlisted leader regardless of the command's mission. I set out to monitor and enforce standards, to ensure our enlisted soldiers were trained and ready to perform their individual and team requirements, and to look out for the welfare of those soldiers and their families. Just as in previous assignments, I knew I had to get out and be among the soldiers. And because of the number of places that our command was located, that often meant traveling long distances.

In joining any new unit the transition is usually always the same. Reassignment to the Space and Missile Defense Command, which was headquartered in a mostly commercial setting and off of a military installation, was a new experience for me. In preparation for my interview and selection, I had begun to study the command to ensure I would know and understand its mission and roles. Beyond what I read, the one thing I knew was that leadership is universal regardless of the setting. I knew and understood what my role was in any organization, but this would be different. Our headquarters was somewhat split: a portion of the staff was located at Redstone Arsenal in Huntsville, Alabama, while other soldiers and units were stationed at a variety of strategic locations. As I embraced my new assignment and joined the ranks of this new command I knew that getting out and being with the men and women of the command—both soldier and civilian—was the most important thing I could do.

A posting in the Washington, DC, metropolitan area has been a unique and wonderful assignment for soldiers since the earliest days of our country. The rich culture and heritage of the United States crisscrosses the landscape of the District and the surrounding states of Virginia and Maryland. Bastions of power like the Capitol, iconic symbols like the Washington Monument, and the never-ending collection of memorials and tributes are testaments of the struggles of those who have led our nation from the earliest days. Our headquarters was located in leased space surrounded by other federal agencies at the Crystal Square 2 building in Arlington, Virginia. During that era, quite often the day-to-day work seemed more academic or corporate than the muddy-boots soldiering that I was accustomed to—but it was still an environment that I enjoyed.

I had arrived during a time when the noncommissioned officer corps as an institution was under intense scrutiny. It seemed that faith and trust in some NCOs was hanging under a dark cloud. The Army was reeling from the backlash of a scandal, first exposed at Aberdeen Proving Ground in Maryland, in which drill sergeants were accused of sexual misconduct. During an investigation it was found similar actions had taken place at other locations and victims were calling in to a specially created hotline in high numbers. In response to the public outcry, the serving Sergeant Major of the Army was directed to join a task force to advise the Secretary of the Army on how to deal with the problem—when he himself was accused of improprieties. He was first suspended, and when a military hearing announced it had grounds to court-martial him, the Chief of Staff of the Army relieved him of his duties. In deciding a replacement, Cmd. Sgt. Maj. Robert E. Hall of the United States Central Command was quickly appointed as his successor, and Hall became the 11th Sergeant Major of the Army. The Army, along with each of the services, needed to nominate one candidate to replace Hall. I was the Army's candidate and was asked to interview for his position even though I had worked just a short amount of time at SMDC.

Lt. Gen. Anderson and I had been working well together, and it was a surprise to us both when I was told I would be nominated. I didn't even know where Central Command, known in military shorthand as CENTCOM, was. Traditionally I should have served 2–3 years with Anderson. I had committed to him and the soldiers of the Space and Missile Defense command, but he saw the value in having me serving at this important command. Shortly thereafter I was summoned to Tampa, FL, to be interviewed by the CENTCOM commander, General Anthony Zinni, USMC. Zinni, a weightlifter and a fellow Vietnam veteran, looked to me like the prototype Marine general. He had great credentials as a warfighter and leader: he had been Director for Operations of the joint task force in Somalia during Operation Restore Hope and had been the commanding general of the 1st Marine Expeditionary Force.

The interview seemingly went very well, and I felt like the general and I had connected. We spoke of our assignments in Vietnam and our families, and after reviewing my career he asked me my thoughts on a few topics. I answered them in my best interviewee manner, but the more we spoke, I saw his genuine concern and passion for what he and his command did. After we said our farewells at the conclusion of the interview I felt good—I just knew I had it in the bag. Soon after the interview I saw Sgt. Maj. of the Army Hall at a change-of-command ceremony, and my heart sank when he didn't even speak to me. I thought for sure that meant I had screwed up the interview somewhere in my conversations with the general. I knew that if the SMA wasn't talking to me that there must be a problem, especially since I had not heard anything about the selection. So I went back to Arlington and told my boss, "General Anderson sir, I am probably going to be with you for a long time." This didn't turn out to be the case: General Zinni called him a few days later and told him that he was going to select me to be his senior enlisted adviser, and that he needed me a week from now to fly with him to the Middle East. After barely six months at SMDC, I had been selected to serve as the CSM of a unified combat command.

Headquartered at MacDill Air Force Base in Tampa, Florida, CENTCOM was the multiservice agency responsible for U.S. operations in the Middle East, Africa, and Central Asia. Though CENTCOM does not have combat forces under its direct command, it directs the service component commands. The commands in which I served in the past were confined to camps, posts, and even the United States, but I now had an area of operation that covered continents. We did this with the fine soldiers, marines, sailors and airmen of the entire Defense Department, and the Coast Guard; my boss, General Zinni, would serve as the president's military representative in the region and would be the senior commander in the event of hostilities. It was the same position General H. Norman Schwarzkopf Jr. occupied during Desert Storm in the early 1990s.

One of the immediate differences I noted as the senior enlisted leader at CENTCOM was my interactions with servicemen and women of the different branches. While in Bosnia-Herzegovina, I had many opportunities to work with other services, but this was the first time I was at a command that they were directly assigned to me and where we worked closely daily. I quickly learned that by "growing up" in one service I had my biases, and that the distinct cultures were often foreign and a source of tension. For my entire tour, I found myself working to build understanding between the services.

One area in which I had trouble finding common ground was with physical fitness. In the Army, we made physical training a priority; good leaders pushed their soldiers hard to maintain top physical conditions because we might be called to fight in any environment on any terrain. But that is not so for sailors, who may operate on confined ships or submarines where strength may be more important than cardio-respiratory endurance. Conditions differ as well: though soldiers and marines operate in the mud and dust and grime, a USAF aircraft repairer may need to operate in a cool and dry environment to protect his multimillion-dollar airframe. My belief was that everyone should do hard rigorous physical training every day. Unfortunately for me not everyone at CENTCOM agreed. But I did take pride in being able to institute a monthly four-mile run for those serving at our Tampa headquarters. I thought of it as a little victory.

Serving outside the traditional Army assignment can be lonely, especially at the top. First off, your service sometimes loses sight of you. I was lucky because the current Sergeant Major of the Army had just left my same position and understood the dynamics, but on the other hand he was 100 percent focused on and concerned with his service duties. I, on the other hand, had to not only work with (and often through) him, but with the other service senior enlisted advisers. Each of them had their own particular service slant for solutions to problems, which made my job even more of a challenge. There are few regulations and policies that govern all services, so as such I had to get smart on them and learn the policies of each service to know how to operate within them. I had to provide advice and counsel to enlisted personnel of all services assigned to CENTCOM, to listen to their feedback and concerns, and reconcile or identify challenges.

When faced with problems, I divided them up and sent them to the staff, except for the very few that actually had to go to Zinni. In the unusual event I couldn't solve a problem I would take it to the boss to get his blessing or to have him make a decision. As a senior enlisted leader you try not to run to the commanding general to fix all your problems, and one of my best techniques was to solve them at the lowest level. If I could help put out a fire before it reached the general I did, but not every situation could be resolved with my style and personality.

Working alongside the service senior enlisted leaders could sometimes be a challenge. The Army was not necessarily any more accommodating than the other services just because I was a soldier. I felt that by being out of the mainstream Army it could be easy to be forgotten about by your own service. Though our headquarters was in Tampa, I would often spend days and weeks overseas in places like Bahrain, Jordan, or Oman—where I was off the Army's radar. But I kept after it. I would often reach out to meet with the services at the Pentagon as well as in our areas of operation, and I would encourage them to visit their service members, with the hopes of working together.

Even after those overtures I would sometimes learn of a senior enlisted leader flying in to a location to meet with his or her troops and leave without ever coordinating between our offices. To me it was a military courtesy, not necessarily one of power or authority. I spent an extraordinary amount of effort trying to communicate with them while creating opportunities to reach out and connect, and in hindsight that connection was never at the level that I had hoped it to be.

Serving alongside a Marine general was a pleasure. General Zinni was a consummate professional and a great strategic thinker, and I learned much about diplomacy from him. I was a bit unsure how he would use me as his sergeant major; however, he gave me the latitude I felt I needed to be successful on his behalf. He agreed that I could be another set of eyes and ears throughout the command. I visited the finest men and women of the U.S. armed forces in some pretty inhospitable places.

On one visit to Bahrain, I traveled with Zinni to meet with our service members. We flew in to the primary airport and traveled by armored vehicles to a secure location where he met with the troops. He toured the site and then held a gathering and made some remarks and answered a few follow-up questions. Having finished his formal part, he was planning to depart when I told him I would catch a ride back; I wanted to hang back and talk to the group who had been milling around. After the general left I assembled the group and told them I thought they were holding back—there were hardly any questions asked—and so I told them there was no way that General Zinni and I could help them if they didn't share their questions and concerns. That broke the ice and the next thing I knew it was almost two hours later. By the time I got back I had pages of notes for General Zinni and the staff.

It wasn't just members of the U.S. military I met with: I represented CENTCOM in meetings with senior sergeants in Middle Eastern and African nations' armies. I would often provide advice and counsel on American systems and how we grew our professional enlisted force, and provided opportunities to exchange systems and programs. As much as I thought I had to learn from and share with my sister services, I learned that the United States and its military are blessed in resources when compared with many of the military forces and coalition partners.

During one multi-nation trip, I was on a military base in a country long forgotten when they gathered their senior sergeants together. Through their interpreter we held an hour-long discussion about shared interests. Often there were pleas or suggestions for ways the United States could fund a project or otherwise infuse cash into their military or economy, but other than that it seemed to be a typical setting. After I said my farewells at the conclusion and departed, I asked the driver to turn around so I could go back. I had left a notepad or something behind and I wanted to grab it.

I walked back in to the same room and I saw there was a meeting going on, but the lights were out and the projector was off. I asked the interpreter what was happening. He explained that there was a briefing going on, but since they had used the electricity allotted to them by briefing me they would have to finish up the remainder in the dark. I was initially taken aback, and it helped me realize that an important resource like electricity may be routine for many Western nations, but such resources were scarce in much of the region that we covered.

I was also quick to learn that other services consider their enlisted force not quite the same as the Army does. The Army has a separate but distinct noncommissioned officer support channel that parallels and complements the formal chain of command, which is distinct and different from the other services. Because of that, enlisted Army leaders at the company, battalion, brigade, and higher levels derive authority and responsibility from their commander, and as such, influence an organization in a service-unique way. That does not always sit well with leaders of the other services, some in the Army included, especially commissioned officers. The USMC has a very similar approach to enlisted leaders and advisers. In my opinion, the Army is more advanced in the level of authority granted to NCOs, and to me it often showed through.

On one trip General Zinni and I were going to back-to-back ceremonies put on by two different services to award decorations to deserving service members. At the time CENTCOM had been undertaking military operations almost continuously since the end of Operation Desert Storm: the "No Fly Zones" in northern and southern Iraq were ongoing, and occasional flare-ups were responded to with operational names like Vigilant Warrior, Vigilant Sentinel, Desert Strike, Desert Thunder, and Desert Fox. These were often in response to an action or threat made by Saddam Hussein's Iraq.

Because of Zinni's role, he often served as a senior official or reviewing officer. There is much about American military tradition and protocols, including a ceremonial style that crosses branch boundaries. These traditions date back to the American Revolution. On one leg, we helicoptered out to a Navy vessel for the general to present some awards. When we arrived, we were met by a Navy captain (0-6) who briefed the general on the sequence of events and what his role was to be. I interjected and asked if there was an enlisted person I could talk with about the ceremony; he explained there wasn't, and that he was it.

I stepped back and watched the ceremony unfold, and in my mind it was a poorly executed, half-assed event. While we were flying back from the ceremony, I told General Zinni as much. We were heading to an Army site next and I had not prompted anyone to react differently than they had planned; I suspected he would see a difference in the precision between the two. As soon as we landed we were met by the host commander and his sergeant major. The CSM briefed the general and I on the sequence and what they expected of Zinni, and then they went right to it. The ceremony went off without a hitch, and during the ride back the general agreed he did spot the difference, and noted how the sergeant major was a major part of the planning and execution of the parade. For us both, identifying the challenges was the easy part— the solutions themselves resided in the services, and it wasn't necessarily our role to fix them.

Those problems were sometimes small and inconsequential when considered against the bigger picture of what we were working to accomplish. As a representative of the combined enlisted force to the commander and his staff, I often felt like I had to defend the role and our authority, and constantly remind leaders of many services and many nations that the enlisted men and women are more than the "subaltern" of days gone by—that junior in grade does not mean "lower," like in the term "lower enlisted."

Soon after I arrived to CENTCOM I attended one of my first commanders' conferences, in which we brought in the subordinate commanders and their enlisted leaders. I went into the empty room beforehand and saw that General Zinni's nametag was at the head of the table and the senior enlisted adviser tag was all the way at the end. Having been accustomed to always sitting next to my commander, when I questioned protocol I was told "that's the way we do it here." Confused, I asked the chief of staff (who was an Army colonel) about it; he said that he didn't want to anger the other services by putting me at the head of the table. I told him I did not want to make a fuss now and asked that he fix it for the future.

A young airman who was setting up the room saw my frustration and asked me if I was unhappy with how the room was set up. I explained what had happened and he asked me to show him. So we walked to the room and I pointed out the nametags and explained that I should be next to the general. He nodded his head in understanding, pushed the other nametags aside, placed mine to the left of the general, and asked "How is this?" I said yes and took my seat just as the others came in to the room; a word was never said about it again. I advised the colonel that at the next meeting he needed a bigger room, and that I expected each senior enlisted adviser to sit next to their boss so they could easily consult with them. It was fixed from that point on.

Understanding Tilley

> When you become a Noncommissioned Officer or Petty Officer, you are then an empowered and trusted leader in America's all-volunteer force. As a leader and technical expert, you enhance organizational effectiveness and directly contribute to mission success. Innovative, adaptive, and resilient, you are the indispensable link between command guidance and execution, ensuring that each task is fully understood and supervised through completion.
>
> —*The Noncommissioned Officer and Petty Officer,*
> *Backbone of the Armed Forces*

Serving in a nontraditional assignment can be especially rewarding, but can also be filled with challenges because of the uniqueness of the position. One of my most eye-opening experiences was working in a joint command where I had interactions with noncommissioned and petty officers of the Army, Marines, Navy, Air Force, and the Coast Guard. As a senior noncommissioned officer my roles and responsibilities did not change much, but I was now at a higher level and dealing with a broader mission and a wider span of control.

In dealing with enlisted soldiers I saw that there were many service differences. Sometimes our service biases can cause unnecessary friction between people. The most important lesson I had to learn was patience in understanding the other service cultures. Something as simple as implementing a command-wide physical fitness program was a challenge for me because each service's standards for measuring fitness was different. (While I was at CENTCOM the service fitness exams expected Marines to run three miles, Soldiers to run two, Sailors to run a mile, and Airmen to ride a stationary bike.) Learning about all those different policies was important, and not understanding the other branches' cultures could come off as an insult to their service, which was not something I wanted to do. It became my responsibility to understand and treat their service rules respectfully without trying to impose my own bias, and to create a program that supported their service's expectation.

While at CENTCOM I often found myself frustrated in dealing with the different service senior enlisted leaders or the staffs at the departmental level, we didn't always see eye-to-eye on challenges or perceived problems. Some of the nuances of service-specific rules often did not mix well in a joint service assignment and occasionally conflict arose. After I retired then-Chairman General Peter Pace, USMC, created a new position to address some of that friction by establishing the senior enlisted adviser to the Chairman of the Joint Chief of Staff. There was talk of a similar position prior to the designation and I had my reservation, I was mostly concerned that the assignment folks had to offer up the best candidates with the right type of personality.

During my tenure, I had no avenue other than the service senior enlisted advisors. To be fair, most problems were not with the individuals who held the offices, but in the policies and procedures that were uniquely service specific. For our command, which had to "conduct operations" in what was and is a volatile region, I sometimes felt like we were in competition for resources and often felt like I was just grasping for support. While I may not have had the influence at the time to better manage the communication channels that existed, I was better informed on the importance of addressing solutions to building better relationships at my next assignment.

[12]

The Pinnacle

"I listen, then, but with thirsty ear for the witching melody of faint bugles blowing reveille, of drums beating the long roll. In my dreams, I hear the crash of guns, the rattle of musketry, the strange mournful mutter of the battlefield." I used those words from General Douglas MacArthur at my departure ceremony on 22 June of 2000 and less than 15 months later there was a different crash of guns, a different rattle of weapons, and another strange mournful mutter of the battlefield. On 9/11 we were faced with the beginning of the Global War on Terrorism. Jack Tilley continued to be with Soldiers as he traveled the world being a forceful advocate for them, whether at training sites and on battlefields, as well as in the Halls of the Pentagon and in his testimonies before Congress.

— Sgt. Maj. of the Army Robert E. Hall,
U.S. Army, Retired
11th Sergeant Major of the Army

June 23, 2000

I never really envisioned myself as Sergeant Major of the Army. I was sure that there was something unique and distinct about the NCOs who were selected for such an important position. I had always held the position in such high esteem that even up to and while I was division sergeant major I had felt that there was more I would need to experience and to know before I would even consider such a position. I just did the job at hand and eventually opportunities opened up for me. When the announcement came out requesting nominations to replace the sitting Sergeant Major of the

Army I knew that I was eligible for consideration, but felt that I would not be considered a viable candidate. One of the biggest reasons was that I was fairly senior: I had over thirty years of service and I would need a waiver if I was selected.

When the Army begins the hunt for a new SMA it releases a service-wide announcement that lists the prerequisites, explains the nomination procedures, and announces a deadline for submission of nomination packets. As the deadline approached I received a call from the Army senior personnel sergeant, Sgt. Maj. Larry Strickland. Larry reminded me the deadline was near and that I needed to hurry and get in my packet. I explained to him that I wasn't going to compete, which he questioned. He realized that I wasn't just delaying and that I really did not plan to submit a packet. A few days later I received a call from SMA Hall, who started the conversation off with "I understand you haven't put in a packet? Submit your packet." I understood, and told him I acknowledged, and then he finished the conversation up with the comment, "Don't worry, they will never hire you." I discussed it with General Zinni, who thought I would be a great candidate, and he nominated me for the position and signed my recommendation.

There were thirteen of us who were finalists for Hall's position. We were from across the Army and all fine soldiers. Among the group was the first female candidate as well as an Active Guard and Reserve sergeant major. We came from across the globe—the Office of the Sergeant Major of the Army coordinated our travels, and it may have been coincidence that when we arrived at Reagan National Airport they were short one seat in the van they had sent to pick us up. I waved off the others and said I would wait for the van to come back. The airport was close to the SMDC headquarters

I served at just a few years before, I knew my way around, so I decided to walk to the Metro rail station to catch a ride to my hotel. The staff seemed a little flabbergasted when they found me walking the streets of the capital with my luggage in tow; an empty van was dispatched to pick me up and transport me to join the group.

A Sergeant Major of the Army nominating board is a lot like a sergeant promotion board, or at least mine was. Lt. Gen. Leon LaPorte was president and he had three major generals, a brigadier, and the outgoing Sergeant Major of the Army as board members; a captain served as recorder but did not vote. The board met at the then Army Personnel Center in the Hoffman II building in Alexandria, Virginia (now the Human Resources Command at Fort Knox). To be considered for Sergeant Major of the Army a command sergeant major needed a minimum of twenty-six years of service, to be able to complete their tour prior to reaching thirty-five years of service, have no commissioned or warrant officer service, and to have successfully served at the general officer level.

The board met face-to-face with the thirteen candidates over two days. I was interviewed on the second day. Each of us had our own set interview time, as one would finish the other would just be arriving, hardly a word was spoken as we passed the other going into board. We were instructed not to talk to each other about the board proceedings, as it might provide someone an unfair advantage. After being told to report, it was as straightforward as any other interview. I reported to the President of the Board, saluted, and took my seat where they told me to. They asked me if I knew why I was there, and once I affirmed then the grilling began. The president wanted me to talk about myself and then the board members quizzed me on why I wanted the position and what I would do in it, and they asked questions relating to the Army as a whole; there were no prepared questions. After what seemed like ten minutes or so, the president dismissed me and said, "We will be in contact with you." I saluted and walked out. That was it.

I went back to my room and after a brief period of time I received a phone call at about 1600. The voice on the phone congratulated me. I already knew by then that I had a good chance, because shortly before my call I saw some of the other candidates outside hailing cabs with their bags in tow, obviously not moving on to the next stage. I was one of the five finalists selected for the next step, which was a personal interview with the Chief of Staff of the Army. I had never served with Gen. Eric K. Shinseki, the 34th Chief of Staff of the Army, but we had met when I was the 1st Armored Division CSM.

He was then a brigadier general in Augsburg, Germany, with the 3rd Infantry Division. We were both attending an Army Europe briefing, and the meeting was brief and casual. Our paths didn't cross again until we were at an Association of the United States Army annual meeting and he was the Vice Chief of Staff. We passed each other in a hallway and I stopped, and then backed up to catch him. Shinseki recognized me and asked, "Hey Sergeant Major Tilley, how are you?" I said, "Not as good as you sir, because you have four stars now and I am still just a sergeant major." We laughed, shook hands, exchanged pleasantries, and then went on our way. The very next time I saw him was May 4, 2000, in a conference room when I was about to interview for the position of Sergeant Major of the United States Army.

The remaining candidates were all seated in a conference room and we met with General Shinseki. He told all of us we were competitive and he said, "any one of you are qualified to be the next Sergeant Major of the Army." After he took the time to thank us, the staff called us off the list alphabetically one by one to have an office call with him; I was fourth in the lineup. We each spent about forty-five minutes with him, a private conversation in which he attempted to learn as much as possible about us and our thoughts. I likened the conversation to him "picking my brain" for thoughts and opinions on a variety of topics. Electronic mail was just starting to become mainstream in the Army and he asked my thoughts about leaders directing orders through e-mail versus face-to-face; he also asked about the types of things I would want to accomplish, and of course he solicited my views on Army Transformation. He was a champion of transforming the Army, and he was convinced that the Army needed to become lighter, modular, and more deployable.

The Army had created Force XXI in the mid-1990s and some of its major initiatives were just now being launched. They were considering a future combat system and there was much discussion about an objective force, called the "Army After Next." Technology was being tested in many arenas and the general wanted to know my thoughts. I told him, "Sir, I can help you sell transformation." I explained how I thought I could be on point to educate soldiers on the transformation process and why it was important to them. He said it didn't need to be sold, and he explained that we could talk transformation for the next four years, but there will still be people in the Army who just don't get it. He asked me my thoughts on where the Army was, on NCO education, as well as other issues at hand. We then wrapped up the conversation with me sharing my vision for a nominative-level command sergeant major conference to bring together the most senior sergeants for updates and briefings.

I knew it was good discussion and I felt positive by the time I left the general's office. The last candidate went in behind me, so I waited with the rest of the group until the general finished with him. SMA Hall was also there. The chief spoke to us one last time, telling us he didn't know who he was going to select as the next Sergeant Major of the Army but that "you are all qualified and I thank you. Whoever is selected I expect all of you to support him." And then he said he would be in touch. We were back in the vans heading our own separate ways. And to wait.

The interview was the end of a hectic week, so when I returned to Tampa I just wanted to unwind. To me this was a good time to recharge. I spent the weekend with Gloria at home and planned to take a little time off the following week. Golf continued to be a release for me, and something I enjoyed doing in my off time whenever I got the chance. I recall being on the second hole at my local course when my phone rang and it was Hall. He told me that I needed to come back to Washington for another interview, this one with the Secretary of the Army. I said, "That must be good, who else is going to be there?" Hall said, "Just you, so don't screw it up."

According to Army regulations the Sergeant Major of the Army is the senior enlisted advisor to the CSA, but the SMA serves "at the discretion of the Secretary of the Army." It was clear that General Shinseki wanted me as his next SMA, but I first had to meet with The Honorable Luis Caldera, the seventeenth Secretary of the Army. The interview was cordial and we had a brief but meaningful conversation. As I was leaving his office, he told me to "tell Sergeant Major Hall that I am giving you a thumbs-up." I had his seal of approval, which I told Hall. He instructed me that I had to keep quiet and I couldn't tell anyone; there would be a formal announcement and I was to return to Tampa and await further instructions.

I was swelled up with pride knowing that I had crossed the final hurdle. The realization was just beginning to set in that I was about to become the 12th Sergeant Major of the Army. I felt as if I was going to burst and couldn't wait to tell someone; I figured the Army wouldn't mind if I told my wife. As soon as I got home I gave Gloria a big kiss and said, "Guess what, I am going to be the next Sergeant Major of the Army." She said "Jack, that's good," but kept working about the house. So I told her again, and I got the same response: "That's good, Jack." It was when I said it a third time that she replied "Congratulations, now the garbage needs to be taken out." Whether she meant to or not she had put it all into perspective to me: I didn't need to start getting full of myself, because I was the same person I was before the announcement. I tried to keep myself busy and as much as possible act like I didn't know the status of the selection. One week later the announcement was made Army-wide and in another week, I was on my way back to the Pentagon to assume my duties as the Sergeant Major of the Army.

Hosted by General Shinseki, the swearing-in ceremony was held on June 23, 2000, in the Hall of Heroes near Corridor 10 on the second floor of the Pentagon. The Hall of Heroes is dedicated to all the recipients of the Medal of Honor, and their names are displayed on the room's walls. Prior to the swearing-in, Gloria and I met with Shinseki and his wife, Patty. Just before 1400 hours they escorted us to our seats, where we were surrounded by some 150 guests. There were friends, family, soldier's past and present, and even a high school friend who made the trip from Vancouver to surprise me. It was an awe-inspiring day. The chief said positive words about both the position and me, and then with my hand placed firmly on a bible he administered the oath of office to me. The Army had saved my life and it was now my turn to give back in ways unimaginable. At that moment, I swore to "well and faithfully execute the duties of the office upon which I am about to enter. So help me God." I took that oath damn seriously.

Very early on, the Chief had given me guidance and direction for what he wanted me to do as his senior enlisted adviser. The specified duties of a Sergeant Major of the Army are limited, as our authority, beyond general military authority and positional authority, comes from the Chief. He told me to watch my lane and to stay focused on noncommissioned officers and soldier responsibilities. He also asked me to be out and about with soldiers and to be on the ground to see what was going on across the force. As in all my previous positions, the role of the noncommissioned officer has always been about accomplishing the organization's mission and the care of soldiers and their families.

As far as I was concerned, being SMA meant that there were new ways to tackle that challenge, such as testifying before Congress or representing the total enlisted force to Army leaders and staff. I could summarize my role and responsibilities as being there to take care of soldiers and their families, to keep people informed, and explaining to groups, inside and outside of the Army, what was happening with their soldiers of the United States Army.

Soon after my selection, my mentor John Stephens told me to be careful not to change: the things that made me who I was helped me to be selected, and so I needed to continue to be myself. Even though I had unrestricted access to General

Shinseki, I soon realized just how busy the Chief of Staff is. Every moment of his day was carefully choreographed by his squad-sized personal staff and though I could walk in at any time, I didn't have to very often. We usually met in his office each Monday where we would sit down and go over the week's events. I could send him my observations and trip reports via e-mail and we would occasionally travel together. Between social receptions, ceremonies, and meetings at the Pentagon and beyond, we had ample time to talk to one other.

I learned early on that few people in the Army had the exposure to all the individual parts that make up the body we call the United States Army. I was one of a handful who had complete access, and purpose, to peek into and report on the operational, the institutional, and the industrial sides of the Army. I had free range to travel to meet with leaders of any command, post, or assignment, and often did. Every commander had access to me, and me to them, and it was a position that I appreciated every day. I traveled almost 800,000 miles to execute my boss's desire for me to be on the ground learning of soldier hardships and rewards.

As the Army's senior sergeant I also had the opportunity to work closely with the other senior service enlisted leaders: the Sergeant Major of the Marine Corps, Master Chief Petty Officer of the Navy, Chief Master Sergeant of the Air Force, and the Master Chief Petty Officer of the Coast Guard. I formed strong ties with a few in particular: SMMC Al McMichael, MCPON Jim Herdt, CMSAF Fred Finch, and MCPOCG Vince Patton. Developing and maintaining relationships with them and their services was instrumental to me. Because of our shared experiences we have formed long-lasting friendships that have extended from our professional lives to our personal ones.

Coming out of CENTCOM and unhappy with some of my experiences I had dealing with their offices from a Combatant Command perspective, I had the plan to build closer ties with my counterparts. We often would appear together in front of Congress and at Department of Defense activities and functions, as well as take part in special events in the National Capitol Region. I also set out to strengthen my relationship with the Army Reserve and the Army National Guard. Each of those components had a command sergeant major appointed and I strived to include them at every opportunity. As I would travel I would visit their sites and meet with their soldiers, taking on issues and concerns that may have been unique or unsolved. I would often take away problems that might have been unique to a guardsman or reservist and had not surfaced at the Department of the Army level. I came to appreciate that the Army could not function without the National Guard and Army Reserve.

A few mentors advised that I should not try to tackle everything in the Army at once—I should focus on a few important efforts and do them very well. As I met with groups of soldiers certain concerns cropped up time and again, which allowed me to hone in on what was important for me to focus on. My "top five" issues were pay, healthcare, housing, quality of life, and operations tempo, but pay inequity topped the list most of the time. This was a tough problem to address because the argument often became derailed when someone would compare officer pay and enlisted pay, as well as civilian education requirements or lack thereof. And because pay is a service entitlement, the conversation and agreements had to occur between all the services.

Pay-inequity concerns continued throughout my tenure and that became one of the areas where I felt I had the greatest impact. After a major review of military pay in 1997 it was determined that the pay tables had changed very little since 1949 and the gap between civilian and military pay in similar professions had grown, with military personnel receiving much less than their civilian counterparts. One issue of concern of mine was that a senior command sergeant major with nearly 30 years in the military earned less than a captain, and that was not a way to entice enlisted soldiers to stick around and make a career in the service.

The service senior enlisted advisers and I contended that an increased number of enlisted soldiers have degrees. The enlisted promotion systems gave a higher weighting to soldiers with degrees and upwards of 15 percent of all noncommissioned officers then had degrees. Some argued that if it was more pay NCOs were after they should get their degree and apply to become an officer; my point was that we should pay them for the job we expect them to perform. Through the work of many people, we were able to gain targeted pay raises for enlisted personnel of all the services during the years 2000-2004.

In an all-volunteer force, when the economy is good there could be fewer high quality enlistees interested in military service, and the Army could end up with a less-qualified force. One way to counter that is through better pay. In 1999 Congress worked to reduce what they called "pay compression," the result of which was across-the-board pay raises. But pay inequities were created by these "all-in" raises because they did not take in to account high performers who advanced quicker than their peers; soldiers were rewarded solely on longevity, not performance. But thanks to the efforts from all the senior enlisted advisors from the services that we were able to voice our concerns. In the end, there were annual and mid-year pay increases. Additionally, a new public law allowed for "targeted" pay raises for promising mid-careerists. By 2004 a sergeant first class with ten years' time in service who had earned $2,294 a month in 2000 now earned $2,891 in basic pay.

I loved every day I was a soldier and being Sergeant Major of the Army was the greatest honor I could have had. I was surrounded by a talented team of noncommissioned officers in the Office of the Sergeant Major of the Army. My Executive Officer, Sgt. Maj. Johnny Myers, was a detailed thinker and problem solver and one to which I owe a debt of gratitude. He was the steady hand that kept the office running. I had a great senior administrator Sgt. 1st Class Pearl Houck who was detailed and efficient and always kept me organized. Travel coordinator S. Sgts. Karen Viegas and Branch Dildine worked tirelessly, while S. Sgt. Sheila Snipes managed issues that came in from the field. I had two top notch public affairs assistants in Master Sgts. Dave Schad and Rich Puckett, who often traveled alongside me and kept my messages in the forefront. Johnny and I worked hard to not only ensure that we had a staff of people with the right skills and who could operate successfully at such a highly visible position, but that was made up of a diverse cross-section of the Army and reflected the soldier population that I represented.

I loved what I was doing, but without a doubt some days were harder than others. Soon after Gloria placed my dress uniform jacket on me at my swearing-in ceremony with the rank of Sergeant Major of the Army, General Shinseki announced in October 2000 that as a symbol of our Army's transformation the standard headgear for most of the Army units would be a black beret. Because one of the groups who wore the black beret at the time had a strong group of veterans lobbying to keep that color for themselves, I spent a lot of time and energy debating the history and traditions of the beret.

The outrage, misinformation, and resistance to change was a quick lesson for me about bureaucracy. As people continued to question the Chief and his motives, the issue eventually ended up at the White House and was subject to review by Deputy Defense Secretary Paul Wolfowitz. In the end the Secretary of Defense concurred with Wolfowitz's opinion and concurred with the Army's decision. Shinseki announced that I would create an implementation plan and that Army leaders planned to complete the change by the Army's birthday in June 2001. The way I figured it was that if you couldn't change your headgear you sure as hell couldn't handle transformation. In the end we all donned our berets on the Army birthday and a new tradition was created. Today soldiers know the Army birthdate and every soldier stands up and sings whenever the Army song is played.

One misstep in transformation came when the Army replaced our twenty-year slogan *Be All You Can Be* with the *Army of One*. It didn't click with soldiers, retirees, and veterans, and it struggled from the beginning. Introduced to the public by a video of a soldier running alone describing the importance of their role. Countless people complained that the Army was a team and service was not about the individual, I heard about it at many of the places I traveled. I received gripes about the "wrong" parts of the message: "This guy is running the wrong way," "He's not in the proper uniform," "Where was his values tag?" and "Where is his plotter team?" Some soldiers and veterans just did not understand that to transform we needed a different message to reach a changing society.

I had to remind them that the recruiting message was not for them, we had them already. It was for the "millennials" were trying to reach and to get them to consider joining the Army. It was difficult to get people to understand—heck, I had to watch the commercial three times without saying anything to begin to understand what the message was. The "Army of One" campaign was not just TV commercials and radio ads; it also brought in web-based technology to better reach a more tech savvy demographic. There was an interactive "Go Army" website while programmers created the "America's Army" game. There were marketing and sponsorship efforts in different markets, exposing new groups to positive messages about the U.S. Army. In the end *Army of One* was short-lived and the succeeding *Army Strong* had been much more successful.

It was through many successful and sometimes wildly popular events that we were able to make the largest impacts. When I came onboard the Sergeant Major of the Army had meetings with a small but trusted group of the most senior sergeants major in the Army. Called the "Sergeant Major of the Army Board of Directors," it was made up of the command sergeants major from the major Army commands and reserve components. They would meet and discuss important issues affecting the Army enlisted force, often making policy-level recommendations. Because of location or assignment, I never had the opportunity to participate in such meetings but I felt there should be more voices added to the discussion; I wanted to open that audience up to a larger cross-section of the force.

I created the Nominative Command Sergeants Major Conference where we brought together sergeants major from the general officer commands of the active, guard, and reserves for an annual 3-to-4 day seminar. It was my way to bring them up to speed on changes in the Army, as well as to gather issues from their respective corners of the Army. These events were well attended, and leaders from the Army Staff—often the principal, and if they had one, their sergeant major—would brief attendees on the state of the Army from their functional area. This was a popular way to quickly disseminate information both up and down the support channel, and it was a place for me to hear many voices in one group setting.

Another milestone was the creation of the Department of the Army Noncommissioned Officer and Soldier of the Year competition. For many camps, posts, and stations the NCO and Soldier of the Year was a local competition that pit soldier against soldier for the honor of being declared "best" for that year. Many competed at selection boards or went through many challenges for that recognition, but there had never been a competition at the Army level between the major commands. Initially in 2002 a panel of the most senior enlisted leaders in the Army tested a soldier's physical endurance, military and current events knowledge, and mental perseverance. There was a hands-on component where candidates we challenged to perform common-skills tasks and their performance was graded against the other candidates.

The competition was an opportunity for warriors to highlight their military skills in a competitive environment and measure how well they performed under stress. By our second board in 2003 it had expanded to a rigorous three-day, hands-on assessment of wartime skills. The competition pitted soldiers and noncommissioned officers of the eleven major commands against a set standard, and only one in each category could be selected. Some of the tasks that the competitors had to master were physical fitness, land navigation, a written exam, common task testing, a foot march with rucksacks, and a mystery event.

The event was graded and scored. The scores in each category were tabulated at the end, and a winner was announced at the Association of the United States Army annual meeting in Washington, DC. For many, participation in this event, and those leading up to their selection to participate, was a career-enhancing challenge. For the very few who have been selected since, it has been most rewarding.

Understanding Tilley

If you want to make enemies, try to change something.
—Woodrow Wilson

Change is hard in any organization, and in a bureaucratic institution like the United States Army it can feel like it is damn near impossible sometimes. Educating and informing the more than one million people in the active, Guard, Reserve, and civilian components about new and emerging policies was a daunting task. The adage that "the only thing constant in the Army is change" probably holds true for every Sergeant Major of the Army; the Army continually tries to grow and improve and I am convinced that my tenure was similar to others before and since.

As I dealt with and reacted to the results of transformation I realized that I had to temper my high expectations. I was not able to quickly transmit information about changing policies and procedures across an organization as large as the U.S. Army. I had to keep myself in check by remembering the difficulty in spreading news to soldiers at every level. I had to give leaders time to react while still imparting a proper sense of urgency.

As change became more frequent and in more areas, I felt that information flow was a challenge. This bugged me. By being at the top of the noncommissioned officer support channel, which is a channel of communication, I felt that often the messages were not being transmitted to soldiers in the field in a manner that I thought was timely. Or, that the information was garbled or not clear enough. I knew the major and functional commands' leaders were sharing information with their subordinates and mostly the next level or two were sharing, but things began to get murky after about Division and Brigade level. I didn't feel the first sergeants were adequately receiving news of change and I confirmed it quite often in my field visits and in my briefings to soldiers.

Key to my efforts was my ability to get out and talk to people. That is where I would receive immediate feedback and discover if what we were doing was making an impact, and I would learn from the young men and women who serve. By talking to groups, large and small, I could get a sense of information flow and I would often always try to bring in news "from inside the Beltway." I would get soldiers to participate in my briefings by asking them about rumors and if they knew of a specific change. Often my gut instinct would tell me if information was being put out correctly, or even if at all.

I also was sensitive to differences in natural gaps in areas like race or gender, as well to changes in society. I knew I couldn't easily identify with eighteen- or twenty-year-olds with diverse backgrounds and experiences outside of my own; heck, I couldn't tell what was cool or hot, let alone the slang. I was a square. For me the only way I knew how to garner their opinions was to get down on the ground and be with and among them so that I could get their perspectives firsthand. I was always asking questions and taking some top-level discussions to the soldiers to get their input so I could take feedback back to the Pentagon.

Technology was aiding in this, but even with the advent of systems like Army Knowledge Online and other electronic tools, they were not always the proper solution. One of the risks about electronic mail, besides over reliance on it, could be in reaching too far down the chain of command while skipping over a whole layer of leaders. In the Army, superiors traditionally work two levels down. When you start going beyond that it runs the risk of micro-management, or at least perceptions of. That, and a whole group of leaders are being left out of an information or decision loop, and issuing orders by email could easily result in that.

Electronic mail was not new to me. I had first started using it as a division sergeant major and my predecessor was known for sharing his e-mail address. I recalled General Shinseki's concerns about over reliance on email during my interview, but I saw how useful forms of digital tools like electronic mail, newsgroups, and online forums were being used more often to flatten organizations and aid in speedier communications. At first there was a resistance to some of them and their use, and often the adoption of these tools was squelched or discouraged. As time has passed most have grown comfortable with some forms of technology in their lives.

[13]

9/11

My first impression of Jack Tilley was through my husband. Larry and I often attended social events hosted by the SMA and you could see his genuine nature on display, from deeply private conversations to spontaneous entertaining moments with a mic in hand. He was a true example of a loving family man, with his wife Gloria and their son Brian a central presence for those gatherings. I spent five years at Fort Belvoir as post CSM during which time my husband was killed at the Pentagon and I struggled with indecision about my future and career. SMA Tilley approached me about a position with a new organization, coaching me to consider that we shared the challenge of leading Soldiers during a stressful time in the Army and that I was a key member of his Army team. That was Jack Tilley—in the midst of chaos he was steadfast and pulling the team together.

—Cmd. Sgt. Maj. Debra L. Strickland, U.S. Army, Retired
former Command Sergeant Major, Installation
Management Command

September 11, 2011

I was sitting at the desk in my Pentagon office, preparing to visit the annual Better Opportunities for Single Soldiers conference, when my public affairs specialist Dave Schad called me and told me I needed to turn on the television set. The news was showing a burning building and was reporting that an airplane had crashed into the top floors of the north tower of the World Trade Center in New York City. The news had been reminding the viewers that the World Trade Center had been a scene of an attack by terrorists in 1993, and my gut instinct told me the events unfolding were deliberate. As I left my Pentagon office I told no one in particular that we shouldn't think that those were accidents. I reminded them that bad people could try to strike out at us even right here. Soon after I left another plane hit the south tower.

My travel coordinator and I loaded into a sedan from the car pool and we headed for nearby Fort Myer, which was just a few minutes away. My meeting there wrapped up fairly quickly and we headed back to my office. We had just crested a hill on the way back to the Pentagon when a plane struck the western side of the building. It happened so fast that I didn't know what it was at first; I assumed it was a fuel cell that had ignited. I told the driver to get me up as close to the area as he could and I hopped out, only to be confronted by a Pentagon security officer.

Security was unusually tight because of the World Trade Center attacks, as events were still unfolding we did not understand the danger that lay ahead. The officer was a big guy with a large belly and he had a machine gun slung across his chest and resting on it. He was not very imposing. He tried to stop me, telling me "You can't go in there." I said back to him, "Oh yeah, well how fast can you run?" I dodged around him and took off toward the billowing smoke. He didn't try to stop me; he must have realized that I was not going to give up so easy.

The Pentagon has five sides, five floors above ground, two basement levels, and five ringed corridors per floor spanning 17-miles. American Airlines Flight 77 struck the Pentagon near the Army and Navy side of a newly renovated area between Corridors 4 and 5. It hit near the helipad, had pierced the outer ring and passed through four of the five rings of offices. I ran through the Pentagon entrance that the

Army staff traditionally used and made my way to my office. I saw that my staff was evacuating and that everybody was accounted for.

The building was still on fire, and thick black smoke was swirling overhead as I exited the building. I ran into Lt. Gen. John A. Van Alstyne, who had been assisting in the evacuation. The area of the building we were at was mostly intact so I followed him back in to the Pentagon to see if we could locate survivors. As we went deeper into the building, the smoke and heat became overpowering. I eventually said to Van Alstyne, who was the deputy assistant secretary of defense for military personnel and had only been at his job for a short time, "Hey sir, we can't breathe in here. You've got to come back. You can't go any farther." He turned around and we both left the building.

By the time we exited the first responders had reached the scene. There were helicopters in the air, and the personnel on the ground were using ambulances, military vehicles, and buses to move people out of one of the busiest office buildings in America. The Red Cross had set up stations and medical personnel were running triage in the parking lots and inner courtyard. Federal response agencies were beginning to assemble and people in general were looking for how they could help. I joined a number of people helping pick through the rubble, collecting and turning over pieces of plane and wreckage. As stories began to emerge from the survivors and we made discoveries of the victims, we learned of the horrors that those inside endured.

As the day wore on word came down that the staff was mobilizing the Old Guard to collect the remains. The Old Guard comprised the units of the 3rd U.S. Infantry Regiment, the country's oldest active-duty regiment; its legacy heralds from the First American Regiment of 1784. The Old Guard is the Army's ceremonial unit and touts such units as the Army Band, the Fife and Drum Corps, and the guards at the Tomb of the Unknown Soldier. Though it had a couple of infantry companies, they were not an infantry regiment in the traditional sense. When I heard the plan I went to the staff and reminded them that we had trained mortuary specialists who were better suited for the delicate task at hand, and that it was in our best interest to allow them to process the scene, which is what they did.

There were twenty-two soldiers, forty-seven Army employees, and six Army contractors who perished that day, including Lt. Gen. Timothy Maude, the Army Deputy Chief of Staff, and his sergeant major, Sgt. Maj. Larry Strickland. Also killed was my comrade Sgt. Maj. Lacey Ivory, with whom I worked closely in navigating the military pay rules. Also lost were fifty-nine civilians, including the six crewmembers aboard American Airlines Flight 77.

I spent most of that day on the scene helping where I could, talking with and consoling others. The Army is a family, and when something like that happens it just tears at your heart. I wanted to be where I thought I could do the most good. Each of the losses was a tragedy for our nation but Strickland was the victim that I had worked closest with. He was on leave that day and really didn't need to be there, but as one of the senior personnel sergeants in the Army he was working on many important enlisted policies, and like so many he was committed to his duties. At one point during the day I was with his wife, Debra, also an active-duty sergeant major, when she asked me if I thought Larry was still alive. There was nothing I could say; the best I could do at the moment was to hug her.

A shock to the nation, 9/11 changed my life and will continue to do so. I will never forget. I made sure I spent time with the soldiers working the scene and those of the mortuary affairs units who were faced with processing those lost at the site. Of all the memories that I have from that day few are as enduring as what I saw in the Pentagon's halls and on the grounds in the hours following the attack: Americans coming to the aid of their fallen comrades. It was exactly what I expected to see. It also changed my outlook on my own mortality. I used to go and be gone a week or two weeks and I'd call my wife whenever I got a chance. But since that horrible day I made sure to call my wife two times a day, or more. In hindsight I realized that had that plane been going a different direction, or if the time had shifted one way or another, that could have been me. The events of 9/11 reminded me that life oftentimes ends quickly.

The tone and tempo of my job as SMA changed as I changed my focus more towards supporting an Army engaged in a Global War on Terrorism—first during the invasion of Afghanistan, and then later in Iraq. After our initial military response, my first order of business was in making sure I made time to visit Walter Reed Army Medical Center and other military hospitals to be with injured soldiers and their families.

Seeing the pain and motivation of wounded soldiers at Walter Reed surprised me. When I talked to wounded warriors and their families it absolutely broke my heart. But it often only seemed sad for me; it wasn't always for them. Many of the wounded I met with would be motivated and pumped up. I was not sure if it was because of me or their outlook on their future. Some just wanted to go back to their units while others were planning their future and looking to get on with their lives. I also made sure I took the time to meet with the hospital staff, who were the important caregivers to these men and women.

The other order of business was in making morale-boosting visits to Afghanistan. I was going there to support soldiers. I felt it was important to show them their country still cared about them and to help them deal with the terms of their deployments. I was able to visit the "Screaming Eagles" of the 101st Airborne Division at Bagram Air Base in mid-August 2002, where I met with soldiers and leaders and talked about how proud our country was of them. Sometimes I would give briefings to large crowds, but I was just as comfortable hanging out at a mess hall playing cards and answering soldiers' questions. I would tell them that they were making a difference whether they could see it or not.

During the buildup in Iraq in 2002 I prepared to travel there to meet with the troops when the Chief asked me about it. He thought it best with everything going on that my visit might become a distraction, not only in pulling people away, but in their responsibility for my protection, so I changed my plans and delayed the trip. But as soon as the ground war ended we agreed it was time to go over as soon as possible to be with soldiers.

When I first assumed duties as the Sergeant Major of the Army, Defense Secretary William Cohen would take entertainers and celebrities overseas during Christmas to entertain the troops, and he would encourage the services' senior enlisted leaders to travel with him and be a part of these events. He presided over four of those trips that besides entertainers included sports figures, congressional leaders, military heroes, an astronaut, and an occasional cowboy or two. They were grand events in which he would visit Army posts, Navy ships, and Air Force bases. Cohen himself would open each show by introducing his entourage, and they would offer words of inspiration, support, and encouragement before the entertainment began. The shows included popular acts of the time, like Mary Chapin Carpenter, Carole King, and Jewel. When Cohen's replacement as secretary, Donald H. Rumsfeld, chose not to follow his tradition, I asked Shinseki if I could continue the tradition.

I had seen first-hand the value in similar USO shows while in Bosnia-Herzegovina when Hillary Clinton brought along a USO troupe, that was my introduction to Sheryl Crowe. The Chief approved my request and had the staff set aside a budget and coordinated for the military transport aircraft we needed. My staff and I set out to coordinate our trip with the USO to ensure we could get performers who wanted to be a part of this. Those who did were great; the time they gave of themselves to be with the troops was a great morale boost.

We had entertainers like Karri Turner, Darryl Worley, Mark Wills, John "Bradshaw" Layfield, Ted Hacker, and Al Franken, just to name a few. It was fortuitous that I linked up with Ted, he was a talent manager and had great connections to the entertainment industry and we would continue to work together throughout the remainder of my career, and beyond. Our USO shows would not have been nearly as successful without his expertise.

Many of the entertainers formed lasting ties to the American soldier through their visits, and some continue to visit today. We formed two Christmas tours that went to Afghanistan, Iraq, Kuwait, and Uzbekistan, and we traveled across the theaters of operation and visited and entertained at a number of bases in each area. I felt honored to be a part of something special and to bring a small piece of home to many service members serving in remote and oftentimes uninviting places. It was during this trip that Darryl Worley was inspired to produce the song "Have You Forgotten," which would eventually become a number-one hit on the country music charts.

As the senior noncommissioned officer of the Army I was the spokesman for more than one million enlisted active, Guard, and Reserve soldiers, and their families. I routinely testified before Congress, so it was important to me to be out among the Army wherever soldiers were. In a little over three and a half years I traveled hundreds of thousands of miles. I was there for the beginning and the initial stages of what would become a long conflict, the Global War on Terrorism. The soldiers I saw were motivated and highly ready and I wanted to ensure they stayed that way, but from my experiences I knew that keeping the edge was tough. I told leaders that they and their soldiers needed to stay focused. Even with all the training and preparation, once you get them to the battle the one thing you all want to do is finish and then to get home, so that's what they're focused on.

As I visited soldiers, I would continue to talk about my top priorities as the Sergeant Major of the Army, but I also shared my experiences from Vietnam and Bosnia. They were faced with an emerging threat called Improvised Explosive Devices (IED); we had similar challenges in Vietnam, where our main supply routes were constantly rigged with roadside bombs. When I was a tank crewman one of my cavalry troop's regular tasks was route clearance, in which we would travel Highway 13 looking for mines or explosives. Even in Bosnia-Herzegovina we had the constant threat of mines, so the Army had been dealing with similar threats for some time.

We had to be innovative, as well. I remember when we were in Saigon during Tet, one of our sister squadrons would string wires on the tanks—not concertina wire[5], just a heavy wire laced in rows on the front of the tank. This was the early version of the slat armor like those used on the Army's wheeled Stryker vehicle as a rocket-propelled grenade trap, which caused the round to detonate before the projectile hits the vehicle, reducing the amount of damage.

As the Army's highest-ranking enlisted soldier, I served as the Army Chief of Staff's personal adviser on all enlisted-related matters, particularly in areas affecting soldier training and quality of life. I led the NCO Corps at the top of the noncommissioned officer support channel, where a major part of my duties was to transmit news and concerns of the Chief of Staff, the department, and other leaders to enlisted personnel. But I also had a duty to pass information in the other direction. I was able to influence Army policies and regulations and I served as a role model and standard-bearer. Even in the midst of conflict, I continued to work on what I saw as my top priorities. So after we cared for our people, honored our fallen, and took care of soldiers and their families, I set out to travel across the Army answering soldiers' questions about 9/11 and tried to provide some context and perspective for the way ahead. But I found myself talking often about what I saw that day.

I also championed soldiers obtaining military and civilian educations to increase benefits and gain more access to improve themselves through education. Because of my own career path and the Army that I served in—where the service did not make education a priority—I wanted to ensure that soldiers had the best noncommissioned officer education system possible. It appeared that on average it took soldiers twelve years to get an associate's degree while serving

---

[5] Concertina wire is a type of barbed or razor wire that is formed in large coils.

on active duty, mostly because of their unusual work hours, field exercises, deployments, and strict limits on the number of credit hours under the Tuition Assistance Program. And even then, if you looked at the average service member who obtained a degree, it would show that he or she had accumulated credits well beyond what typically would be required for that degree. I knew I wanted to see that change.

I was also concerned about our aging infrastructure and even painted for Congress a bleak picture of street after street of run-down family housing units at practically every installation I had visited. In my last assignment at CENTCOM I was afforded a modest home of 1,100 square feet, something that I felt was not very fitting for a senior military leader. In my mind it sent a wrong message—we wanted to encourage soldiers to reenlist and make a career of the military, but in some areas like housing there were limited incentives. In some places the Army didn't show greater incentives for enlisted leaders with increased responsibility.

Through the efforts of a lot of people, the Army community has seen vast amounts of new construction and renovation at many installations under the Residential Communities Initiative, a great program. I had looked at RCI houses—both new ones and older units being managed by contractors—and I talked to soldiers and families living in the quarters. I believe the RCI houses were the best, largest, and most thoughtfully designed I had seen in all my years of service. I continued to advocate for increases in housing allowances.

Medical care was often a hot topic for soldiers and families and initially I heard numerous complaints about TRICARE, the military health care program. The 2003 National TRICARE Conference invited the services senior enlisted advisors to take part in the efforts to improve health care, and included a panel discussion featuring the top NCOs of each service. It was through events like this that we opened up new communication channels and made progress as changes were made throughout military healthcare. Thanks to increased funding and changes in management, I heard fewer complaints about medical care in general and TRICARE in particular.

January 15, 2004

Are you ready? It was a question people were constantly asking me ever since Command Sergeant Major Kenneth O. Preston had been selected as the 13th Sergeant Major of the Army. He had been serving as the command sergeant major for V Corps in Heidelberg, Germany, and had deployed to Iraq as the CSM of Combined Joint Task Force 7. I would tell anyone who asked that I wasn't sure if you can ever be 100 percent ready. The time had come for me to say so long. I loved being a soldier, but without my wife, Gloria, I know my successes would have ended long ago. There were long deployments, hard separations, tough living conditions, painful losses, and horrible events along the way. I watched friends and fellow soldiers die defending the nation they loved.

It got harder and harder to lose parts of my family as casualties continued to mount overseas. Despite some of the harsh realities of a nation at war, having the privilege to serve as the sergeant major of the entire United States Army was the most satisfying experience I could have ever asked for. I was blessed with an incredible family; Gloria was my rock, I had two terrific and outstanding sons and a wonderful daughter-

in-law, and two precious granddaughters. It had been such
an honor to have served as Sergeant Major of the Army and I
took satisfaction in knowing that I had made a difference in
the lives of the people. Any success I had as the 12th sergeant
major of the army was a direct result of the soldiers I served
with, and I worked with two tremendous officers at the helm
of the Army, Gen. Eric Shinseki and Gen. Peter Schoomaker.
Thanks to those two, I knew the soldier's voice was heard
loud and clear in every decision they made.

During my tour soldiers received higher basic pay and
for the first time in Army history a sergeant major earned
more than a captain. I was an advocate for improving
quality of life initiatives and refining TRICARE programs
supporting soldiers and family members. I also furthered
educating soldiers at NCO Education System (NCOES)
courses and championed classes on retirement benefits and
financial planning. We established the Department of the
Army–level Soldier and NCO of the Year competition to
highlight the Army's best warriors. Even with all this, I left
very concerned about the Army's high operations tempo
and its impact on families, safety, and the NCOES. I saw
330,000 soldiers forward deployed at 120 different locations,
along with 150,000 Reserve soldiers that had been activated.
There was a tremendous amount of stress placed on soldiers
and family members at the time I retired, and I knew my
work was not yet complete.

I left the Army and began my transition on January 15,
2004, after a small ceremony. My swan song event was my
second Middle East USO tour, my third trip to Iraq and
sixth visit to Afghanistan in two years. I wanted people to
know that I tried as hard as I could. To me, it's not about
what you take with you, it's what you leave behind, and I

felt I had left the Army in good hands. I wasn't sure that I knew what I had accomplished on the day I left and I knew it would take a few years to see the results. For me, the true test of my legacy was in watching things unfold the first few years after I retired. In the end, I felt that I carried the ball a few yards farther and was sure the next Sergeant Major of the Army would do the same.

Understanding Tilley

Don't simply retire from something; have something to retire to.
—Harry Emerson Fosdick

I used to tell military leaders that once a month you ought to try to do something with your family. Dedicate time to doing something special with your spouse and/or children to create lasting memories. Don't be afraid to ask for some time off to go to your child's football game or a basketball game. If you tell your family that you're going to do something, do it. Being a soldier is so much different than a civilian career; the last fifteen or so years that I was in the Army I was a sergeant major and I was always gone. It is a difficult lifestyle and you must save time and energy for your family, and that includes parents and siblings.

Soon after I retired I asked Gloria, "What was the last vacation we ever went on?" She thought about it for a moment and said, "Do you remember that AAFES conference we went to a few years ago?" I could not remember the last vacation we were on, and it struck me it was when we went to Myrtle Beach; I was a staff sergeant then. That was it. So how do you endure a lengthy career and not have vacation time when one of your annual benefits is a month of vacation memories? Here is how, I would just collect my vacation days and not use them, oftentimes losing days at the end of every year. Or I would have excess leave, and so I would just put myself on leave—but then go to the office the entire time. It was a tough realization for me, I considered what I had lost in those sacrifices. Even today I ask myself why?

It's important that you do things with your family while you still can. If you have thirty days, take a couple of weeks off. Take a break and allow your family to be part of your life. It feels as if one day you are eighteen and living it up, and in what seems a blink of an eye you have become an old man.

It is up to you to ensure that you make time for your family and to take time off to recharge your batteries. You are allotted leave time, be sure to use them. You may not be in a position to take all thirty days at one time; however, it's important to split up the days to make sure you have adequate time to rest and recuperate. Army leaders often find themselves keeping a hectic pace and you could find yourself burnt out and less effective to your organization. When you are overworked and tired you are more likely to be irritable and want to lash out, plus no one wants to live or work with someone who is always angry. You must practice making time for yourself and your family, and to set an example for living a full family life for your subordinates as well. If leaders do not make time for their families it often becomes a norm, and others may end up copying that trait.

You cannot always control those above you and their actions when it comes to family time. When possible you need to protect those under your charge from bad habits when it comes to setting aside time to replenish yourself and your relationships. The key is, do something with your family and allow your family to be part of your life. If not, one day you find yourself alone and the only thing you have remaining is a heap of missed opportunities and regret.

EPILOGUE

Transition

I had always admired Jack Tilley for the rapport that he developed with soldiers, and nothing more confirmed my beliefs than one particular action at the conclusion of unit-level maneuvers. The Division leadership was hosting an after-action review for a unit at a local training center and as we wrapped up and walked towards the vehicles someone asked about the whereabouts of the Sergeant Major. I knew to look to where I heard a loud, gathering crowd and saw Jack had the soldiers from the review surrounding him while he was enthusiastically cheering and shouting, revving up the group. He had this incredible ability to reach soldiers in a way that allowed them to open up and confide in him where they might not have with somebody else.

—Maj. Gen. Robert R. Hicks, U.S. Army, Retired,
former Assist. Div. Cdr., 1st Armored Division

Soon after I retired, I served as the senior enlisted adviser to the sergeant major of the Afghan National Army. I was also part of the U.S. Army's retirement board and the Secretary of Veterans Affairs' special advisory committee for operations Enduring Freedom and Iraqi Freedom. Seeing the pain—and the often startling level of motivation—of wounded soldiers at Walter Reed Army Medical Center led me to co-create the not-for-profit American Freedom Foundation (AFF), which raises money and awareness for veteran organizations helping wounded soldiers. My experience coordinating entertainment opportunities in Bosnia, and later the USO trips, were a spark that lit the fire that convinced me to continue using entertainment to spread messages of support. It was through a partnership with the entertainment expert

Ted Hacker, who had worked with me on the earlier USO trips, which we came up with the concept for AFF. Ted and I had become close, I consider him one of my personal friends and he is a patriot in his own right. The American Freedom Foundation serves and supports veterans, military service members, and their families by creating awareness of their service and sacrifice and building support through partnerships with military-focused organizations. Even today we continue to "entertain the troops," while raising support, awareness, and resources for soldiers and their families.

I also started my own company specializing in placing today's noncommissioned officers (and commissioned officers) into corporate America, and we provide honorably separated NCOs with career transition employment opportunities. My company and I are also part of a unique joint venture called Pinnacle Five, which links five former top senior enlisted leaders and our respective companies to educate businesses and the American public on the significant value veterans bring to the workplace.

I also became the Co-Chairman of the Army Chief of Staff's Retiree Council, replacing retired Sergeant Major of the Army Robert Hall. The CSA Retiree Council was established November 10, 1971, originally as two separate enlisted and officer councils; these were merged in 1990. All retired service members are represented by similar councils comprising the various armed services: Navy (representing Navy and Marine Corps retirees), Air Force, and Coast Guard. As council cochairman, I represented retired soldiers and families at the council's annual meeting, and I met with retirees at events such as installation Retiree Appreciation Days. I have since completed that four-year term.

Today I give motivational speeches on team building and leader development, focusing on some of the areas I think are often taken for granted. I speak about the things that have touched my life: war, family separation, God, and the fact that America has seen more than 6,800 American soldiers killed in today's wars. Veterans' employment issues are of top concern for me. Though the figures go up and down as our national attention shifts, post–9/11 veterans faced an unemployment rate that was typically higher than that for both veterans of other eras and non-veterans. After nearly fifteen years of war our veterans and their families still need help finding jobs. Soldiers have given so much to our country that it is only right that we help provide opportunities for employment as a way to give something back to them.

For those contemplating leaving the service, I believe that you need to start getting serious about retirement at two years out. I think everybody around their fifteenth year in service should have a resume; you then need to continue to improve upon it while you build on your education and credentials as you get older and more experienced. Finish that degree, get that certification, and make your resume as strong as you can. Collect business cards and contacts from people at least a year out before you retire, and hold on to them.

Those business cards are contacts, so start networking now to help yourself later. When you get ready to get out of the service—about six months out—send those contacts a copy of your resume and let them know your intentions. Reach out to the retiree community, you should find yourself a mentor who has already made the transition. A retiree or two that you feel comfortable with can be an invaluable resource sharing their experiences leaving the service. Pay all your bills off, or pay them down as much as you can. Your income will change, so you must be prepared for that reality. It is important that you are able to get out of the service without a bunch of bills, because in many cases you cannot live on your retirement pay alone.

At two years out you should start developing contacts for jobs. Use professional networking sites like LinkedIn, and make sure your profile is as accurate as your resume. You might not yet be able to sign an offer letter but you surely can talk to people about future employment. Be aware that unless you are in a contracting specialty, enlisted soldiers do not necessarily have the same restrictions that officers do when it comes to "revolving door" rules. Be sure to check with your ethics counselor if you are in the position to have one.

Having been retired for more than ten years, I strongly believe that the service branches need to better prepare mid-grade and senior enlisted service members on how to retire from the service. For some NCOs that is difficult because it's hard to pull back. Every individual is a little different, but for me the first year I was out of the service was a hell of an adjustment. You may not be as good outside the military as you were inside, and sometimes people get wound up and are uncomfortable back in civilian life. It is a certain type of personality that is drawn to serve a career as a senior Army leader, whether it is "Type A," an introvert, or some other personality indicator. But you still must know how to effectively communicate with people outside the military who have never worn the uniform.

Being well prepared to get out of the service should be first and foremost among your considerations. There are plenty of ways to make money, but enlisted soldiers do not always have the same opportunities as their officer counterparts. There are many factors on why that is true. A general officer, a colonel, or a lieutenant colonel are typically more financially prepared to transition than many enlisted soldiers. Whether you made it to 1st Sergeant or Sergeant Major by the time you retire, you cannot sit on your ass very long to decompress; you have to get a job. My team and I have spent the last ten years coaching people on how to successfully transition from the military and my suggestions come from observing many people—some who got it right, and others who had a difficult time.

Too many transitioning senior noncommissioned officers cannot "get out of the Army" or are unable to assimilate back in to a purely civilian culture. This is often because of the mindset we adopt, which sometimes becomes completely pro-military, almost anti-civilian. We literally forget how to be a contributing member of society because of that isolation. It's the one thing that often hinders us in our post-military career—at least until we figure out different approaches.

Some do so at a high cost and some never figure it out. It's not something we can easily fix from the outside and military leaders don't always have the perspective they need to understand the need. What I find to be a contradiction is the idea that the Army trains you to a certain level for thirty-plus years of service and then when you retire and walk out the door it sometimes feels to me that you are forgotten. You have to prepare yourself for the idea that you may still want to remain connected to your service, but the military will likely not need you. The challenge may be that there are so many great leaders to choose from to use everybody, but to me it appears that poor usage of retired soldiers is a great waste of talent.

One bit of advice that I have for any soldier is to complete as much civilian education as you can while you are in the service using your military education benefits. Get a college degree before you ever get out of the service. Junior NCOs and enlisted soldiers who plan one hitch or two should have at least an associate's degree when they separate. It's easier than you think because many schools give you credit for military training and will likely allow you to transfer credits to their college. Mid-grade NCOs should have at least an undergraduate degree or a sought-after technical or professional trade certification in a transferrable skill that will still be needed.

Don't assume a skill that's hot today will be just as hot when you transition; plan ahead as much as possible. And 1st Sergeants and Sergeants Major should consider a graduate degree in a field they hope to enter upon retirement—without one it could mean a 30,000–50,000-dollar difference in the amount of annual pay. And make sure you only deal with accredited institutions, preferably military-friendly ones. Committing yourself to maximizing your education benefits while in the service might allow you an advanced degree, or to transfer your hard-earned GI Bill benefits to your family.

The civilian sector needs people with leadership experience and professional soldiers often have many years of it in difficult assignments. In my case, I entered the service at age seventeen and went straight to Vietnam. I've been a battalion, brigade, and division sergeant major, and I've led a lot of soldiers and trained a lot of troops. I had the type of knowledge and expertise that the civilian sector is desperate for. Veteran NCOs have a wide variety of skills, but a lot of times when we transition from the military we don't value ourselves very well or we haven't properly prepared. It is up to you to know how your skills can be adapted from military use to corporate America.

Talk to people you know and trust about their transition; just as in the military. And don't just talk to one person, talk to a lot of people. There are many who have gone before you and succeeded, so it's not that hard. Remember that you're not alone in your transition: I had prepared Gloria for the time when I would get out of the Army, warning that it would be really hard for me. I had been a soldier for a long time and I would be going through a lot of adjustments. And she looked me in the eye and she said, "You know, I've been in the Army a long time too and I'm going to go through a lot of adjustments when *we* get out of the Army." So, understand that you are not the only one affected by retirement, but your spouse and your family is too. We tend to focus on "me" instead of "we" in transition; remember that when you eventually retire, it's the family ties that will hold it all together.

One regret I have about my own transition is that I should have done a few things differently when it comes to my health. I should have gotten a thorough pre-separation physical. I felt I was too busy and didn't give it the attention it deserved and I realized later that I might have done myself and my family a disservice. I worked up to my final day in the Army because I was a good soldier, and who was going to tell me to slow down or pause? Another factor to consider when it comes to retirement is where do you want to live? The two biggest questions a soldier wants answered before he or she separates is "What is my job going to be?" and "Where am I going to live?" See if you can get assigned somewhere close to where you want to retire. This becomes even more crucial if you have school-age kids, or older children who want to attend college near you.

Living around a military installation is not a bad thing. For some it's good because there will be a lot of people who have similar experiences and you could find yourself living among peers and contemporaries. I settled close to a military installation: I now live twenty-four miles from an Air Force base. Though I still have access to many of my earned benefits, there is not a whole lot of Army veterans nearby. There is something to be said about living among your comrades, even if it is just to stay connected. I have the utmost respect for those who can immerse themselves back in to civilian life, but location is a factor that must be a major consideration as you separate.

Understanding Tilley

Thank you Sergeant Major Tilley for your leadership and values that have made our Army the most professional and effective fighting force in the world. Thank you for your ability to inform the Appropriations Committee on quality of life issues that impact soldiers and their families, and God's blessings to you as you begin your next great journey upon your retirement from the Army.
—Congressional Record Volume 150, Number 2, Wednesday, January 21, 2004

I will be a soldier until the day I die. You can take me out of the military, but you can't take the military out of me. I am a soldier for life. After more than thirty-five years in the military I could not fathom suddenly saying "I quit," and I sure as hell could not get soldiering out of my heart. Nobody really teaches you how to retire, or at least they didn't teach me. And unfortunately, it's something you only get to do once. Though I had left the Army for two years after Vietnam, I realized that had been a mistake and I came back to what I loved doing. I was determined that my second separation was going to be different, now the choices and decisions I made would have long-lasting effects.

At the time that I retired, the Army Career and Alumni Program was in place, but that was well before the program underwent a major overhaul after the passage of the 2011 Veterans Opportunity to Work to Hire Heroes Act, which mandated pre-separation counseling, veteran's benefits briefings, and Department of Labor workshops for all soldiers. But just as now, many of those programs are targeted to a different and more junior soldier population than senior noncommissioned officers with a lifetime of service. There is value in sitting down and talking to experts who understand how to successfully transition from the service, but who could really do that for a Sergeant Major of the Army? The same holds true for other senior enlisted positions; the unique role the American noncommissioned officer performs does not often translate clearly to the civilian workplace.

Was it fun being a solider? Hell yes. I feel blessed when I go back and start listing all the crazy shit I've done in my life. I can't say enough about how proud I am to have been a soldier. Since I retired from the Army I realize I sometimes get sad when I see soldiers in uniform or while traveling. It was truly a gloomy day for me when I took off my uniform for the last time and I realized I wasn't going to be able to wear it again. Now when I see soldiers in places like the airport I think, "I wish I could do that again."

Also, by retiring I realized that I am not in the "circle" any longer, and that there are always new leaders who step right up and fill your shoes. Gen. Douglas MacArthur quoted from the song that says old soldiers "just fade away," but that is something that I find hard to do. Even though people continued to be polite and honor my service, I missed the Army every day for the first six or seven months. Eventually the Army as your full-time life begins to fade, and you can't do much about it but cope. And don't worry about me: I am a soldier for life and I plan to have fun and keep moving forward. Keep your eyes peeled looking for me because this old soldier is not planning on fading away any time soon.

AFTERWORD

I have shared a number of stories and events from my life and my more than thirty-five-year career in uniform. I want to close with some final words of advice and rules to live by not only on how to be a better soldier, but also to assist you in your eventual transition out of the Army and back in to society. Good luck, and remember you are a Soldier for Life, too:

HOW TO BE A SUCCESSFUL NONCOMMISSIONED OFFICER

- ◉ Enforce the Standards—Ensure all military/mission requirements are understood, adhered to, and acted upon

- ◉ Leadership—Provide purpose, direction and motivation, while operating to accomplish the mission and improve the organization (award publicly and reprimand privately)

- ◉ Discipline—Demand uniform cooperation in order to attain a common goal

- ◉ Uniform Policy—Understand and stay abreast of all regulatory requirements

- ◉ Continuing Education—Pursue civilian undergraduate and graduate studies to enhance your military training

- ◉ Formal/Informal Mentoring—Be receptive to guidance and direction from leaders within and outside the chain of command

- ◉ Define "What right looks like"—identify the correct courses of action and utilize them as a compass to remain consistent with mission objectives

- ◉ Enhance strengths and overcome weaknesses—Develop progressive formal and informal training regiment

- ◉ Career-enhancing assignments and schools—Identify a military training curriculum that best identifies objectives

- ◉ Develop a 3-5-year plan—Articulate the objectives that you aspire to

- ◉ Counseling—Ensure goals and objectives are clearly received by superiors and given to subordinates (communication above and below)

- ◉ Development of subordinates—Provide future leaders the proper tools to achieve success

- ◉ Lead by example—Always do the right thing, on and off duty; someone is always observing

- ◉ Understand diversity—Appreciate cultural differences and incorporate those that enhance development

- ◉ Effective communication with officers—Respect, Respect, and Respect. Provide guidance when requested and become that invaluable trusted advisor

- ◉ Don't become the enlisted General—Recognize placement within the organization and don't become excessively ambitious or arrogant

HOW TO TRANSITION FROM THE MILITARY

- ⦿ Finances—Pay off outstanding debt, create savings (six-month cushion)

- ⦿ Education—Achieve at least an associate's degree, work towards certifications, obtain undergrad and graduate degrees (enhance your marketability)

- ⦿ Housing/Relocation—Determine housing requirements and desires, and find a location that fits your needs

- ⦿ Health/Dental care—Review options, costs, and desired level of care in accordance with your situation

- ⦿ Insurance—Review options, costs, and desired level of coverage—ensure a decision is quickly determined with VSGLI

- ⦿ VA—Begin the disability review process as early as possible and ensure medical records are updated prior to initiating the process

- ⦿ Take at least a thirty-day break—This means both a mental and physical break

- ⦿ Create your resume at the 15-year career mark— Modify the document as accomplishments and educational achievements are met

- ⦿ Emphasize the importance of the transition program—Physically attend all transition training as soon as possible, obtaining knowledge of options and potential opportunities for advancement within the public and private sector

- Take advantage of separate transition courses for senior NCO and officers at the executive leadership level—Get access to knowledge-based training and education for managerial positions within the public and private sectors

- Employment and career goals (two years prep—one year resume—understand offer letter) friends, know your value—identify proper attire—job interviews should be viewed as Army boards (keep question direct and to the point)

- Establish timeline—Develop a checklist prior to retirement/separation, ensuring all objectives are met

- Networking—Retain contacts for potential job opportunities

- Establish your value—Do your homework and evaluate your skills, education, and training. Do not overestimate or underestimate yourself

- Family process—The most valuable team; ensure all members' voices are considered

- Save leave—This will provide a significant financial cushion prior to the separation/retirement date

Made in the USA
Coppell, TX
05 November 2019

11036598R00134